England and the War

England and the War

being

SUNDRY ADDRESSES

delivered during the war
and now first collected

by

WALTER RALEIGH

Essay Index Reprint Series

BOOKS FOR LIBRARIES PRESS, INC.
FREEPORT, NEW YORK

First Published 1918
Reprinted 1967

LIBRARY OF CONGRESS CATALOG NUMBER:
67-30228

PRINTED IN THE UNITED STATES OF AMERICA

CONTENTS

PREFACE

THIS book was not planned, but grew out of the troubles of the time. When, on one occasion or another, I was invited to lecture, I did not find, with Milton's Satan, that the mind is its own place; I could speak only of what I was thinking of, and my mind was fixed on the War. I am unacquainted with military science, so my treatment of the War was limited to an estimate of the characters of the antagonists.

The character of Germany and the Germans is a riddle. I have seen no convincing solution of it by any Englishman, and hardly any confident attempt at a solution which did not speak the uncontrolled language of passion. There is the same difficulty with the lower animals; our description of them tends to be a description of nothing but our own loves and hates. Who has ever fathomed the mind of a rhinoceros; or has remembered, while he faces the beast, that a good rhinoceros is a pleasant member of the community in which his life is passed ? We see only the folded hide, the horn, and the angry little eye. We know that he is strong and cunning, and that his desires and instincts are inconsistent with our welfare. Yet a rhinoceros is a simpler creature than a German, and does not trouble our thought by conforming, on occasion, to civilized standards and humane conditions.

It seems unreasonable to lay great stress on racial differences. The insuperable barrier that divides England from Germany has grown out of circumstance and habit and thought. For many hundreds of years the German peoples have stood to arms in their own defence against the encroachments of successive empires; and modern Germany learned the doctrine of the omnipotence of force by prolonged suffering at the hands of the greatest master of that immoral school—the Emperor Napoleon. No German can understand the attitude of disinterested patronage which the English mind quite naturally assumes when it is brought into contact with foreigners. The best example of this superiority of attitude is to be seen in the people who are called pacifists. They are a peculiarly English type, and they are the most arrogant of all the English. The idea that they should ever have to fight for their lives is to them supremely absurd. There must be some mistake, they think, which can be easily remedied once it is pointed out. Their title to existence is so clear to themselves that they are convinced it will be universally recognized; it must not be made a matter of international conflict. Partly, no doubt, this belief is fostered by lack of imagination. The sheltered conditions and leisured life which they enjoy as the parasites of a dominant race have produced in them a false sense of security. But there is something also of the English strength and obstinacy of character in their self-confidence, and if ever Germany were to conquer England some of them would spring to their full stature as the heroes of an age-long and indomitable resistance. They are not held in much esteem to-day among their own people; they are useless for the work in hand; and their credit has suffered from the multitude of pretenders who make principle a cover for cowardice. But for all that, they are kin to the makers of England, and the fact that Germany would never tolerate them for an instant is not without its lesson.

We shall never understand the Germans. Some of their traits may possibly be explained by their history. Their passionate devotion to the State, their amazing vulgarity, their worship of mechanism and mechanical efficiency, are explicable in a people who are not strong in individual character, who have suffered much to achieve union, and who have achieved it by subordinating themselves, soul and body, to a brutal taskmaster. But the convulsions of war have thrown up things that are deeper than these, primaeval things, which, until recently, civilization was believed to have destroyed. The old monstrous gods who gave their names to the days of the week are alive again in Germany. The English soldier of to-day goes into action with the cold courage of a man who is prepared to make the best of a bad job. The German soldier sacrifices himself, in a frenzy of religious exaltation, to the War-God. The filthiness that the Germans use, their deliberate befouling of all that is elegant and gracious and antique, their spitting into the food that is to be eaten by their prisoners, their defiling with ordure the sacred vessels in the churches—all these things, too numerous and too monotonous to describe, are not the instinctive coarsenesses of the brute beast; they are a solemn ritual of filth, religiously practised, by officers no less than by men. The waves of emotional exaltation which from time to time pass over the whole people have the same character, the character of savage religion.

If they are alien to civilization when they fight, they are doubly alien when they reason. They are glib and fluent in the use of the terms which have been devised for the needs of thought and argument, but their use of these terms is empty, and exhibits all the intellectual processes with the intelligence left out. I know nothing more distressing than the attempt to follow any German argument concerning the War. If it were merely wrong-headed, cunning, deceitful, there might still be some compensation in its cleverness. There is no such compensation. The statements made are not false, but empty; the arguments used are not bad, but meaningless. It is as if they despised language, and made use of it only because they believe that it is an instrument of deceit. But a man who has no respect for language cannot possibly use it in such a manner as to deceive others, especially if those others are accustomed to handle it delicately and powerfully. It ought surely to be easy to apologize for a war that commands the whole-hearted support of a nation; but no apology worthy of the name has been produced in Germany. The pleadings which have been used are servile things, written to order, and directed to some particular address, as if the truth were of no importance. No one of these appeals has produced any appreciable effect on the minds of educated Frenchmen, or Englishmen, or Americans, even among those who are eager to hear all that the enemy has to say for himself. This is a strange thing; and is perhaps the widest breach of all. We are hopelessly separated from the Germans; we have lost the use of a common language, and cannot talk with them if we would.

We cannot understand them; is it remotely possible that they will ever understand us? Here, too, the difficulties seem insuperable. It is true that in the past they have shown themselves willing to study us and to imitate us. But unless they change their minds and their habits, it is not easy to see how they are to get near enough to us to carry on their study. While they remain what they are we do not want them in our neighbourhood. We are not fighting to anglicize Germany, or to impose ourselves on the Germans; our work is being done, as work is so often done in this idle sport-loving country, with a view to a holiday. We wish to forget the Germans; and when once we have policed them into quiet and decency we shall have earned the right to forget them, at least for a time. The time of our respite perhaps will not be long. If the Allies defeat them, as the Allies will, it seems as certain as any uncertain thing can be that a mania for imitating British and American civilization will take possession of Germany. We are not vindictive to a beaten enemy, and when the Germans offer themselves as pupils we are not likely to be either enthusiastic in our welcome or obstinate in our refusal. We shall be bored but concessive. I confess that there are some things in the prospect of this imitation which haunt me like a nightmare. The British soldier, whom the German knows to be second to none, is distinguished for the levity and jocularity of his bearing in the face of danger. What will happen when the German soldier attempts to imitate that? We shall be delivered from the German peril as when Israel came out of Egypt, and the mountains skipped like rams.

The only parts of this book for which I claim any measure of authority are the parts which describe the English character. No one of purely English descent has ever been known to describe the English character, or to attempt to describe it. The English newspapers are full of praises of almost any of the allied troops other than the English regiments. I have more Scottish and Irish blood in my veins than English; and I think I can see the English character truly, from a little distance. If, by some fantastic chance, the statesmen of Germany could learn what I tell them, it would save their country from a vast loss of life and from many hopeless misadventures. The English character is not a removable part of the British Empire; it is the foundation of the whole structure, and the secret strength of the American Republic. But the statesmen of Germany, who fall easy victims to anything foolish in the shape of a theory that flatters their vanity, would not believe a word of my essays even if they were to read them, so they must learn to know the English character in the usual way, as King George the Third learned to know it from Englishmen resident in America.

A habit of lying and a belief in the utility of
lying are often attended by the most unhappy and
paralysing effects. The liars become unable to recognize the truth when it is presented to them. This
is the misery which fate has fixed on the German
cause. War, the Germans are fond of remarking, is
war. In almost all wars there is something to be
said on both sides of the question. To know that
one side or the other is right may be difficult; but it
is always useful to know why your enemies are
fighting. We know why Germany is fighting; she
explained it very fully, by her most authoritative
voices, on the very eve of the struggle, and she has
repeated it many times since in moments of confidence
or inadvertence. But here is the tragedy of Germany:
she does not know why we are fighting. We have
told her often enough, but she does not believe it,
and treats our statement as an exercise in the cunning
use of what she calls ethical propaganda. Why ethics,
or morals, should be good enough to inspire sympathy,
but not good enough to inspire war, is one of the
mysteries of German thought. No German, not even
any of those few feeble German writers who have
fitfully criticized the German plan, has any conception
of the deep, sincere, unselfish, and righteous anger
that was aroused in millions of hearts by the cruelties
of the cowardly assault on Serbia and on Belgium.
The late German Chancellor became uneasily aware
that the crucifixion of Belgium was one of the causes
which made this war a truceless war, and his
offer, which no doubt seemed to him perfectly reasonable, was that Germany is willing to bargain about

Belgium, and to relax her hold, in exchange for solid advantages elsewhere. Perhaps he knew that if the Allies were to spend five minutes in bargaining about Belgium they would thereby condone the German crime and would lose all that they have fought for. But it seems more likely that he did not know it. The Allies know it.

There is hope in these clear-cut issues. Of all wars that ever were fought this war is least likely to have an indecisive ending. It must be settled one way or the other. If the Allied Governments were to make peace to-day, there would be no peace; the peoples of the free countries would not suffer it. Germany cannot make peace, for she is bound by heavy promises to her people, and she cannot deliver the goods. She is tied to the stake, and must fight the course. Emaciated, exhausted, repeating, as if in a bad dream, the old boastful appeals to military glory, she must go on till she drops, and then at last there will be peace.

These may themselves seem boastful words; they cannot be proved except by the event. There are some few Englishmen, with no stomach for a fight, who think that England is in a bad way because she is engaged in a war of which the end is not demonstrably certain. If the issues of wars were known beforehand, and could be discounted, there would be no wars. Good wars are fought by nations who make their choice, and would rather die than lose what they are fighting for. Military fortunes are notoriously variable, and depend on a hundred accidents. Moral causes are constant, and operate all the time. The chief of these moral causes is the character of a people. Germany, by her vaunted study of the art and science of war, has got herself into a position where no success can come to her except by way of the collapse or failure of the English-speaking peoples. A study of the moral causes, if she were capable of making it, would not encourage her in her old impious belief that God will destroy these peoples in order to clear the way for the dominion of the Hohenzollerns.

MIGHT IS RIGHT

First published as one of the Oxford Pamphlets, October 1914

IT is now recognized in England that our enemy in this war is not a tyrant military caste, but the united people of modern Germany. We have to combat an armed doctrine which is virtually the creed of all Germany. Saxony and Bavaria, it is true, would never have invented the doctrine; but they have accepted it from Prussia, and they believe it. The Prussian doctrine has paid the German people hand-somely; it has given them their place in the world. When it ceases to pay them, and not till then, they will reconsider it. They will not think, till they are compelled to think. When they find themselves face to face with a greater and more enduring strength than their own, they will renounce their idol. But they are a brave people, a faithful people, and a stupid people, so that they will need rough proofs. They cannot be driven from their position by a little paper shot. In their present mood, if they hear an appeal to pity, sensibility, and sympathy, they take it for a cry of weakness. I am reminded of what I once heard said by a genial and humane Irish officer con-cerning a proposal to treat with the leaders of a Zulu rebellion. 'Kill them all,' he said, 'it's the only thing they understand.' He meant that the Zulu chiefs would mistake moderation for a sign of fear. By the irony of human history this sentence has become almost true of the great German people, who built up the structure of modern metaphysics. They can be argued with only by those who have the will and the power to punish them.

The doctrine that Might is Right, though it is true, is an unprofitable doctrine, for it is true only in so broad and simple a sense that no one would dream of denying it. If a single nation can conquer, depress, and destroy all the other nations of the earth and acquire for itself a sole dominion, there may be matter for question whether God approves that dominion; what is certain is that He permits it. No earthly governor who is conscious of his power will waste time in listening to arguments concerning what his power ought to be. His right to wield the sword can be challenged only by the sword. An all-powerful governor who feared no assault would never trouble himself to assert that Might is Right. He would smile and sit still. The doctrine, when it is propounded by weak humanity, is never a statement of abstract truth; it is a declaration of intention, a threat, a boast, an advertisement. It has no value except when there is some one to be frightened. But it is a very dangerous doctrine when it becomes the creed of a stupid people, for it flatters their self-sufficiency, and distracts their attention from the difficult, subtle, frail, and wavering conditions of human power. The tragic question for Germany to-day is what she can do, not whether it is right for her to do it. The

buffaloes, it must be allowed, had a perfect right to
dominate the prairie of America, till the hunters came.
They moved in herds, they practised shock-tactics,
they were violent, and very cunning. There are but
few of them now. A nation of men who mistake
violence for strength, and cunning for wisdom, may
conceivably suffer the fate of the buffaloes, and perish
without knowing why.

To the English mind the German political doctrine
is so incredibly stupid that for many long years, while
men in high authority in the German Empire, ministers,
generals, and professors, expounded that doctrine at
great length and with perfect clearness, hardly any one
could be found in England to take it seriously, or to
regard it as anything but the vapourings of a crazy
sect. England knows better now; the scream of the
guns has awakened her. The German doctrine is to
be put to the proof. Who dares to say what the result
will be? To predict certain failure to the German
arms is only a kind of boasting. Yet there are guarded
beliefs which a modest man is free to hold till they
are seen to be groundless. The Germans have taken
Antwerp; they may possibly destroy the British fleet,
overrun England and France, repel Russia, establish
themselves as the dictators of Europe—in short, fulfil
their dreams. What then? At an immense cost of
human suffering they will have achieved, as it seems
to us, a colossal and agonizing failure. Their engines
of destruction will never serve them to create anything
so fair as the civilization of France. Their uneasy
jealousy and self-assertion is a miserable substitute
for the old laws of chivalry and regard for the weak,

which they have renounced and forgotten. The will and high permission of all-ruling Heaven may leave them at large for a time, to seek evil to others. When they have finished with it, the world will have to be remade.

We cannot be sure that the Ruler of the world will forbid this. We cannot even be sure that the destroyers, in the peace that their destruction will procure for them, may not themselves learn to rebuild. The Goths, who destroyed the fabric of the Roman Empire, gave their name, in time, to the greatest mediaeval art. Nature, it is well known, loves the strong, and gives to them, and to them alone, the chance of becoming civilized. Are the German people strong enough to earn that chance? That is what we are to see. They have some admirable elements of strength, above any other European people. No other European army can be marched, in close order, regiment after regiment, up the slope of a glacis, under the fire of machine guns, without flinching, to certain death. This corporate courage and corporate discipline is so great and impressive a thing that it may well contain a promise for the future. Moreover, they are, within the circle of their own kin, affectionate and dutiful beyond the average of human society. If they succeed in their worldly ambitions, it will be a triumph of plain brute morality over all the subtler movements of the mind and heart.

On the other hand, it is true to say that history shows no precedent for the attainment of world-wide power by a people so politically stupid as the German people are to-day. There is no mistake about this;

the instances of German stupidity are so numerous
that they make something like a complete history of
German international relations. Here is one. Any
time during the last twenty years it has been matter
of common knowledge in England that one event, and
one only, would make it impossible for England to
remain a spectator in a European war—that event
being the violation of the neutrality of Holland or
Belgium. There was never any secret about this, it
was quite well known to many people who took no
special interest in foreign politics. Germany has
maintained in this country, for many years, an army
of spies and secret agents; yet not one of them
informed her of this important truth. Perhaps the
radical difference between the German and the English
political systems blinded the astute agents. In England
nothing really important is a secret, and the amount
of privileged political information to be gleaned in
barbers' shops, even when they are patronized by Civil
servants, is distressingly small. Two hours of sympathetic conversation with an ordinary Englishman would
have told the German Chancellor more about English
politics than ever he heard in his life. For some reason
or other he was unable to make use of this source of
intelligence, so that he remained in complete ignorance
of what every one in England knew and said.

Here is another instance. The programme of German
ambition has been voluminously published for the
benefit of the world. France was first to be crushed;
then Russia; then, by means of the indemnities pro-
cured from these conquests, after some years of
recuperation and effort, the naval power of England

was to be challenged and destroyed. This programme
was set forth by high authorities, and was generally
accepted; there was no criticism, and no demur. The
crime against the civilization of the world foreshadowed
in the horrible words ' France is to be crushed ' is before
a high tribunal; it would be idle to condemn it here.
What happened is this. The French and Russian part
of the programme was put into action last July.
England, who had been told that her turn was not
yet, that Germany would be ready for her in a matter
of five or ten years, very naturally refused to wait
her turn. She crowded up on to the scaffold, which
even now is in peril of breaking down under the
weight of its victims, and of burying the executioner
in its ruins. But because England would not wait
her turn, she is overwhelmed with accusations of
treachery and inhumanity by a sincerely indignant
Germany. Could stupidity, the stupidity of the wise
men of Gotham, be more fantastic or more monstrous ?

German stupidity was even more monstrous. A part
of the accusation against England is that she has raised
her hand against the nation nearest to her in blood.
The alleged close kinship of England and Germany is
based on bad history and doubtful theory. The English
are a mixed race, with enormous infusions of Celtic and
Roman blood. The Roman sculpture gallery at Naples
is full of English faces. If the German agents would
turn their attention to hatters' shops, and give the
barbers a rest, they would find that no English hat
fits any German head. But suppose we were cousins,
or brothers even, what kind of argument is that on
the lips of those who but a short time before were

explaining, with a good deal of zest and with absolute
frankness, how they intended to compass our ruin?
There is something almost amiable in fatuity like
this. A touch of the fool softens the brute.

The Germans have a magnificent war-machine which
rolls on its way, crushing all that it touches. We shall
break it if we can. If we fail, the German nation is
at the beginning, not the end, of its troubles. With
the making of peace, even an armed peace, the war-
machine has served its turn; some other instrument
of government must then be invented. There is no
trace of a design for this new instrument in any of
the German shops. The governors of Alsace-Lorraine
offer no suggestions. The bald fact is that there is no
spot in the world where the Germans govern another
race and are not hated. They know this, and are
disquieted; they meet with coldness on all hands, and
their remedy for the coldness is self-assertion and brag.
The Russian statesman was right who remarked that
modern Germany has been too early admitted into the
comity of European nations. Her behaviour, in her
new international relations, is like the behaviour of
an uneasy, jealous upstart in an old-fashioned quiet
drawing-room. She has no genius for equality; her
manners are a compound of threatening and flattery.
When she wishes to assert herself, she bullies; when
she wishes to endear herself, she crawls; and the one
device is no more successful than the other.

Might is Right; but the sort of might which enables
one nation to govern another in time of peace is very
unlike the armoured thrust of the war-engine. It is
a power compounded of sympathy and justice. The

English (it is admitted by many foreign critics) have studied justice and desired justice. They have inquired into and protected rights that were unfamiliar, and even grotesque, to their own ideas, because they believed them to be rights. In the matter of sympathy their reputation does not stand so high; they are chill in manner, and dislike all effusive demonstrations of feeling. Yet those who come to know them know that they are not unimaginative ; they have a genius for equality ; and they do try to put themselves in the other fellow's place, to see how the position looks from that side. What has happened in India may perhaps be taken to prove, among many other things, that the inhabitants of India begin to know that England has done her best, and does feel a disinterested solicitude for the peoples under her charge. She has long been a mother of nations, and is not frightened by the problems of adolescence.

The Germans have as yet shown no sign of skill in governing other peoples. Might is Right; and it is quite conceivable that they may acquire colonies by violence. If they want to keep them they will have to shut their own professors' books, and study the intimate history of the British Empire. We are old hands at the business; we have lost more colonies than ever they owned, and we begin to think that we have learnt the secret of success. At any rate, our experience has done much for us, and has helped us to avoid failure. Yet the German colonial party stare at us with bovine malevolence. In all the library of German theorizing you will look in vain for any explanation of the fact that the Boers are, in the main, loyal to the British Empire.

If German political thinkers could understand that
political situation, which seems to English minds so
simple, there might yet be hope for them. But they
regard it all as a piece of black magic, and refuse to
reason about it. How should a herd of cattle be driven
without goads? Witchcraft, witchcraft!

Their world-wide experience it is, perhaps, which has
made the English quick to appreciate the virtues of
other peoples. I have never known an Englishman
who travelled in Russia without falling in love with the
Russian people. I have never heard a German speak
of the Russian people without contempt and dislike.
Indeed the Germans are so unable to see any charm in
that profound and humane people that they believe that
the English liking for them must be an insincere pretence, put forward for wicked or selfish reasons. What
would they say if they saw a sight that is common in
Indian towns, a British soldier and a Gurkha arm in
arm, rolling down the street in cheerful brotherhood?
And how is it that it has never occurred to any of them
that this sort of brotherhood has its value in Empire-
building? The new German political doctrine has bidden
farewell to Christianity, but there are some political
advantages in Christianity which should not be over-
looked. It teaches human beings to think of one another
and to care for one another. It is an antidote to the
worst and most poisonous kind of political stupidity.

Another thing that the Germans will have to learn
for the welfare of their much-talked Empire is the value
of the lone man. The architects and builders of the
British Empire were all lone men. Might is Right;
but when a young Englishman is set down at an

outpost of Empire to govern a warlike tribe, he has to do a good deal of hard thinking on the problem of political power and its foundations. He has to trust to himself, to form his own conclusions, and to choose his own line of action. He has to try to find out what is in the mind of others. A young German, inured to skilled slavery, does not shine in such a position. Man for man, in all that asks for initiative and self-dependence, Englishmen are the better men, and some Germans know it. There is an old jest that if you settle an Englishman and a German together in a new country, at the end of a year you will find the Englishman governor, and the German his head clerk. A German must know the rules before he can get to work.

More than three hundred years ago a book was written in England which is in some ways a very exact counterpart to General von Bernhardi's notorious treatise. It is called *Tamburlaine*, and, unlike its successor, is full of poetry and beauty. Our own colonization began with a great deal of violent work, and much wrong done to others. We suffered for our misdeeds, and we learned our lesson, in part at least. Why, it may be asked, should not the Germans begin in the same manner, and by degrees adapt themselves to the new task? Perhaps they may, but if they do, they cannot claim the Elizabethans for their model. Of all men on earth the German is least like the undisciplined, exuberant Elizabethan adventurer. He is reluctant to go anywhere without a copy of the rules, a guarantee of support, and a regular pension. His outlook is as prosaic as General von Bernhardi's

or General von der Goltz's own, and that is saying
a great deal. In all the German political treatises
there is an immeasurable dreariness. They lay down
rules for life, and if they be asked what makes such
a life worth living they are without any hint of an
answer. Their world is a workhouse, tyrannically
ordered, and full of pusillanimous jealousies.

It is not impious to be hopeful. A Germanized
world would be a nightmare. We have never at-
tempted or desired to govern them, and we must not
think that God will so far forget them as to permit
them to attempt to govern us. Now they hate us,
but they do not know for how many years the
cheerful brutality of their political talk has shocked
and disgusted us. I remember meeting, in one of the
French Mediterranean dependencies, with a Prussian
nobleman, a well-bred and pleasant man, who was
fond of expounding the Prussian creed. He was said
to be a political agent of sorts, but he certainly learned
nothing in conversation. He talked all the time, and
propounded the most monstrous paradoxes with an
air of mathematical precision. Now it was the
character of Sir Edward Grey, a cunning Machiavel,
whose only aim was to set Europe by the ears and
make neighbours fall out. A friend who was with
me, an American, laughed aloud at this, and protested,
without producing the smallest effect. The stream
of talk went on. The error of the Germans, we were
told, was always that they are too humane; their
dislike of cruelty amounts to a weakness in them.
They let France escape with a paltry fine, next time
France must be beaten to the dust. Always with

a pleasant outward courtesy, he passed on to England. England was decadent and powerless, her rule must pass to the Germans. 'But we shall treat England rather less severely than France,' said this bland apostle of Prussian culture, 'for we wish to make it possible for ourselves to remain in friendly relations with other English-speaking peoples.' And so on—the whole of the Bernhardi doctrine, explained in quiet fashion by a man whose very debility of mind made his talk the more impressive, for he was simply parroting what he had often heard. No one criticized his proposals, nor did we dislike him. It all seemed too mad ; a rather clumsy jest. His world of ideas did not touch our world at any point, so that real talk between us was impossible. He came to see us several times, and always gave the same kind of mesmerized recital of Germany's policy. The grossness of the whole thing was in curious contrast with the polite and quiet voice with which he uttered his insolences. When I remember his talk I find it easy to believe that the German Emperor and the German Chancellor have also talked in such a manner that they have never had the smallest opportunity of learning what Englishmen think and mean.

While the German doctrine was the plaything merely of hysterical and supersensitive persons, like Carlyle and Nietzsche, it mattered little to the world of politics. An excitable man, of vivid imagination and invalid constitution, like Carlyle, feels a natural predilection for the cult of the healthy brute. Carlyle's English style is itself a kind of epilepsy. Nietzsche was so nervously sensitive that everyday life was an anguish to him, and broke his strength. Both were poets, as Marlowe was a poet, and both sang the song of Power. The brutes of the swamp and the field, who gathered round them and listened, found nothing new or unfamiliar in the message of the poets. 'This', they said, 'is what we have always known, but we did not know that it is poetry. Now that great poets teach it, we need no longer be ashamed of it.' So they went away resolved to be twice the brutes that they were before, and they named themselves Culture-brutes.

It is difficult to see how the world, or any considerable part of it, can belong to Germany, till she changes her mind. If she can do that, she might make a good ruler, for she has solid virtues and good instincts. It is her intellect that has gone wrong. Bishop Butler was one day found pondering the problem whether, a whole nation can go mad. If he had lived to-day what would he have said about it? Would he have admitted that that strangest of grim fancies is realized?

It would be vain for Germany to take the world; she could not keep it; nor, though she can make a vast number of people miserable for a long time, could she ever hope to make all the inhabitants of the world miserable for all time. She has a giant's power, and does not think it infamous to use it like a giant. She can make a winter hideous, but she cannot prohibit the return of spring, or annul the cleansing power of water. Sanity is not only better than insanity; it is much stronger, and Might is Right.

Meantime, it is a delight and a consolation to Englishmen that England is herself again. She has

a cause that it is good to fight for, whether it succeed
or fail. The hope that uplifts her is the hope of
a better world, which our children shall see. She
has wonderful friends. From what self-governing
nations in the world can Germany hear such messages
as came to England from the Dominions oversea?
'When England is at war, Canada is at war.' 'To
the last man and the last shilling, Australia will
support the cause of the Empire.' These are simple
words, and sufficient; having said them, Canada and
Australia said no more. In the company of such
friends, and for the creed that she holds, England
might be proud to die; but surely her time is not yet.

Our faith is ours, and comes not on a tide;
And whether Earth's great offspring by decree
Must rot if they abjure rapacity,
Not argument, but effort shall decide.
They number many heads in that hard flock,
Trim swordsmen they push forth, yet try thy steel;
Thou, fighting for poor human kind, shalt feel
The strength of Roland in thy wrist to hew
A chasm sheer into the barrier rock,
And bring the army of the faithful through.

THE WAR OF IDEAS

*An Address to the Royal Colonial Institute,
December 12, 1916*

I HOLD, as I daresay you do, that we are at a crisis of
our history where there is not much room for talk. The
time when this struggle might have been averted or won
by talk is long past. During the hundred years before
the war we have not talked much, or listened much, to
the Germans. For fifty of those years at least the head
of waters that has now been let loose in a devastating
flood over Europe was steadily accumulating; but we
paid little attention to it. People sometimes speak of
the negotiations of the twelve days before the war as if
the whole secret and cause of the war could be found
there; but it is not so. Statesmen, it is true, are the
keepers of the lock-gates, but those keepers can only
delay, they cannot prevent an inundation that has great
natural causes. The world has in it evil enough, and
darkness enough. But it is not so bad and so dark that
a slip in diplomacy, a careless word, or an impolite
gesture, can instantaneously, as if by magic, involve
twenty million men in a struggle to the death. It is
only clever, conceited men, proud of their neat little
minds, who think that because they cannot fathom the
causes of the war, it might easily have been prevented.
I confess I find it difficult to conceive of the war in
terms of simple right and wrong. We must respect the
tides, and their huge unintelligible force teaches us to
respect them.

It is not a war of race.   For all our differences with
the Germans, any cool and impartial mind must admit
that we have many points of kinship with them.   During
the years before the war our naval officers in the
Mediterranean found, I believe, that it was easier to
associate on terms of social friendship with the Austrians
than with the officers of any other foreign navy.   We
have a passionate admiration for France, and a real
devotion to her, but that is a love affair, not a family
tie.   We begin to be experienced in love affairs, for
Ireland steadily refuses to be treated on any other foot-
ing.   In any case, we are much closer to the Germans
than they are to the Bulgarians or the Turks.   Of these
three we like the Turks the best, because they are
chivalrous and generous enemies, which the Germans
are not.

It is a war of ideas.   We are fighting an armed
doctrine.   Yet Burke's use of those words to describe
the military power of Revolutionary France should warn
us against fallacious attempts to simplify the issue.
When ideas become motives and are filtered into
practice, they lose their clearness of outline and are
often hard to recognize.   They leaven the lump, but the
lump is still human clay, with its passions and prejudices, its pride and its hate.   I remember seeing in a
provincial paper, in the early days of the war, two
adjacent columns, both dealing with the war.   The first
was headed 'A Holy War' and set forth the great
principles of nationality, respect for treaties, and pro-
tection of the weak, which in our opinion are the main
motives of the Allies in this war.   The second was
headed 'The War on Commerce; Tips to capture

German trade', and set forth those other principles and
motives which, in the opinion of the Germans, brought
England into this war.

I am not going to defend England against the charge
that she entered this war on a cold calculation of mer-
cantile profit. Every one here knows that the charge is
utterly untrue. Those who believe the charge could
not be shaken in their belief except by being educated
all over again, and introduced to some knowledge of
human nature. It is enough to remark that this charge
is a commonplace between belligerent nations. They all
like to believe that their adversaries entertain only base
motives, while they themselves act only on the loftiest
ideal promptings. If the charge means only that every
nation at war is bound to think of its own interests, to
conserve its own strength, and to seize on all material
gains that are within its reach, the charge is true and
harmless. When two angry women quarrel in a back
street, they commonly accuse each other of being amor-
ous. They might just as well accuse each other of
being human. The charge is true and insignificant. So
also with nations; they all cherish themselves and seek
to preserve their means of livelihood.

If this were their sole concern, there would be few
wars; certainly this war, which is desolating and im-
poverishing Europe, would be impossible. No one,
surely, can look at the war and say that nations are
moved only by their material interests. It would be
more plausible to say that they are too little moved by
those interests. Bacon, in his essay *Of Death*, remarks
that the fear of death does not much affect mankind.
'There is no passion in the mind of man so weak, but

it mates and masters the fear of death; and therefore death is no such terrible enemy when a man hath so many attendants about him that can win the combat of him. Revenge triumphs over death; love slights it; honour aspireth to it; grief flieth to it, fear pre-occupateth it; nay, we read, after Otho the Emperor had slain himself, pity (which is the tenderest of affections) provoked many to die out of mere compassion to their sovereign, and as the truest sort of followers.' If this is true of the fear of death, how much truer it is of the love of material gain. Any whim, or point of pride, or fixed idea, or old habit, is enough to make a man or a nation forgo the hope of profit and fight for a creed.

The German creed is by this time well known. Before the war we took little notice of it. We sometimes saw it stated in print, but it seemed to us too monstrous and inhuman to be the creed of a whole people. We were wrong; it was the creed of a whole people. By the mesmerism of State education, by the discipline of universal military service, by the pride of the German people in their past victories, and by the fears natural to a nation that finds enemies on all its fronts, an absolute belief in the State, in war as the highest activity of the State, and in the right of the State to enslave all its subjects, body and soul, to its purposes, had become the creed of all those diverse peoples that are united under the Prussian Monarchy. Most of them are not naturally warlike peoples. They have been lured, and frightened, and drilled, and bribed into war, but it is true to say that, on the whole, they enjoy fighting less than we do. One of the truest remarks ever made on the war was that famous remark

of a British private soldier who was telling how his
company took a trench from the enemy.   Fearing that
his account of the affair might sound boastful, he added,
' You see, Sir, they're not a military people, like we
are.'   Only the word was wrong, the meaning was
right.   They are, as every one knows, an enormously
military people, and, if they want to fight at all, they
have to be a military people, for the vast majority of
them are not a warlike people.   A first-class army
could never have been fashioned in Germany out of
volunteer civilians, like our army on the Somme.   That
army has a little shaken the faith of the Germans in
their creed.   Again I must quote one of our soldiers :
' I don't say ', he remarked, ' that our average can run
rings round their best ; what I say is that our average is
better than their average, and our best is better than
their best.'   The Germans already are uneasy about
their creed and their system, but there is no escape for
them ; they have sacrificed everything to it ; they have
impoverished the mind and drilled the imagination of
every German citizen, so that Germany appears before
the world with the body of a giant and the mind of a
dwarf ; they have sacrificed themselves in millions that
their creed may prevail, and with their creed they must
stand or fall.   The State, organized as absolute power,
responsible to no one, with no duties to its neighbour,
and with only nominal duties to a strictly subordinate
God, has challenged the soul of man in its dearest
possessions.   We cannot predict the course of military
operations ; but if we were not sure of the ultimate issue
of this great struggle, we should have no sufficient
motive for continuing to breathe.   The State has

challenged the soul of man before now, and has always been defeated. A miserable remnant of men and women, tied to stakes or starved in dungeons, have before now shattered what seemed an omnipotent tyranny, because they stood for the soul and were not prompted by vanity or self-regard. They had great allies—

> 'Their friends were exultations, agonies,
> And love, and man's unconquerable mind.'

If we are defeated we shall be defeated not by German strength but by our own weakness. The worst enemy of the martyr is doubt and the divided mind, which suggests the question, 'Is it, after all, worth while?' We must know what we have believed. What do we stand for in this war? It is only the immovable conviction that we stand for something ultimate and essential that can help us and carry us through. No war of this kind and on this scale is good enough to fight unless it is good enough to fail in. 'The calculation of profit', said Burke, 'in all such wars is false. On balancing the account of such wars, ten thousand hogsheads of sugar are purchased at ten thousand times their price. The blood of man should never be shed but to redeem the blood of man. It is well shed for our family, for our friends, for our God, for our country, for our kind. The rest is vanity; the rest is crime.'

The question I have asked is a difficult question to answer, or, rather, the answer is not easy to formulate briefly and clearly. Most of the men at the front know quite well what they are fighting for; they know that it is for their country, but that it is also for their kind —for certain ideals of humanity. We at home know that we are at war for liberty and humanity. But these words are invoked by different nations in different senses; the Germans, or at least most of them, have as much liberty as they desire, and believe that the highest good of humanity is to be found in the prevalence of their own ideas and of their own type of government and society. No abstract demonstration can help us. Liberty is a highly comparative notion; no one asks for it complete. Humanity is a highly variable notion; it is interpreted in different senses by different societies. What we are confronted by is two types of character, two sets of aims, two ideals for society. There can be no harm in trying to understand both.

The Germans can never be understood by those who neglect their history. They are a solid, brave, and earnest people, who, till quite recent times, have been denied their share in the government of Europe. In the sixteenth century they were deeply stirred by questions of religion, and were rent asunder by the Reformation. Compromise proved futile; the small German states were ranked on this side or on that at the will of their rulers and princes; men of the same race were ranged in mortal opposition on the question of religious belief, and there was no solution but war. For thirty years in the seventeenth century the war raged. It was conducted with a fierceness and inhumanity that even the present war has not equalled. The civilian population suffered hideously. Whole provinces were desolated and whole states were bereaved of their men. When, from mere exhaustion, the war came to an end, Germany lay prostrate, and the chief gains of the war fell to the rising monarchy of France, which had

intervened in the middle of the struggle. By the Treaty
of Westphalia in 1648 Alsace and Lorraine went to
France, and the rule of the great monarch, Louis XIV,
had nothing to fear from the German peoples. The
ambitions of Germany, for long after this, were mainly
cosmopolitan and intellectual. But political ambitions,
though they seemed almost dead, were revived by the
hardy state of Prussia, and the rest of Germany's history,
down to our own time, is the history of the welding of
the Germanic peoples into a single state by Prussian
monarchs and statesmen.

This history explains many things. If a people has
a corporate memory, if it can learn from its own sufferings, Germany has reason enough to cherish with a
passionate devotion her late achieved unity. And German brutality, which is not the less brutality because
Germans regard it as quite natural and right, has its
origin in German history. The Prussian is a Spartan,
a natural brute, but brutal to himself as well as to
others, capable of extremes of self-denial and self-
discipline. From the Prussians the softer and more
emotional German peoples of the South received the
gift of national unity, and they repaid the debt by
extravagant admiration for Prussian prowess and hardi-
hood, which had been so serviceable to their cause. The
Southern Germans, the Bavarians especially, have developed a sort of sentimentalism of brutality, expressed
in the hysterical Hymn of Hate (which hails from
Munich), expressed also in those monstrous excesses
and cruelties, surpassing anything that mere insensibility
can produce, which have given the Bavarian troops their
foul reputation in the present war.

The last half century of German history must also
be remembered. Three assaults on neighbouring states
were rewarded by a great increase of territory and of
strength. From Denmark, in 1864, Prussia took
Schleswig-Holstein. The defeat of Austria in 1866
brought Hanover and Bavaria under the Prussian
leadership ; Alsace and Lorraine were regained from
France in 1870. The Prussian mind, which is not
remarkable for subtlety, found a justification in these
three wars for its favourite doctrine of frightfulness.
That doctrine, put briefly, is that people can always be
frightened into submission, and that it is cheaper to
frighten them than to fight them to the bitter end.
Denmark was a small nation, and moreover was left
utterly unsupported by the European powers who had
guaranteed her integrity. Bavaria was frightened, and
will be frightened again when her hot fit gives way to
her cold fit. France was divided and half-hearted
under a tinsel emperor. It is Germany's misfortune
that on these three special cases she based a general
doctrine of war. A very little knowledge of human
nature—a knowledge so alien to her that she calls it
psychology and assigns it to specialists—would have
taught her that, for the most part, human beings when
they are fighting for their homes and their faith cannot
be frightened, and must be killed or conciliated. The
practice of frightfulness has not worked very well in
this war. It has steeled the heart of Germany's enemies.
It has produced in her victims a temper of hate that
will outlive this generation, and will make the small
peoples whom she has kicked and trampled on impossible subjects of the German Empire. Worst of all,

it has suggested to onlookers that the people who have so plenary a belief in frightfulness are not themselves strangers to fear. There is an old English proverb, hackneyed and stale three hundred years ago, but now freshened again by disuse, that the goodwife would never have looked for her daughter in the oven unless she had been there herself.

How shall I describe the English temper, which the Germans, high and low, learned and ignorant, have so profoundly mistaken? You can get no description of it from the Englishman pure and simple ; he has no theory of himself, and it bores him to hear himself described. Yet it is this temper which has given England her great place in the world and which has cemented the British Empire. It is to be found not in England alone, but wherever there is a strain of English blood or an acceptance of English institutions. You can find it in Australia, in Canada, in America; it infects Scotland, and impresses Wales. It is everywhere in our trenches to-day. It is not clannish, or even national, it is essentially the lonely temper of a man independent to the verge of melancholy. An admirable French writer of to-day has said that the best handbook and guide to the English temper is Defoe's romance of *Robinson Crusoe*. Crusoe is practical, but is conscious of the over-shadowing presence of the things that are greater than man. He makes his own clothing, teaches his goats to dance, and wrestles in thought with the problems suggested by his Bible. Another example of the same temper may be seen in Bunyan's *Pilgrim's Progress*, and yet another in Wordsworth's *Prelude*. There is no danger that

English thought will ever underestimate the value and meaning of the individual soul. The greatest English literature, it might almost be said, from Shakespeare's *Hamlet* to Browning's *The Ring and the Book*, is concerned with no other subject. The age-long satire against the English is that in England every man claims the right to go to heaven his own way. English institutions, instead of subduing men to a single pattern, are devised chiefly with the object of saving the rights of the subject and the liberty of the individual. 'Every man in his humour' is an English proverb, and might almost be a statement of English constitutional doctrine. But this extreme individualism is the right of all, and does not favour self-exaltation. The English temper has an almost morbid dislike of all that is showy or dramatic in expression. I remember how a Winchester boy, when he was reproached with the fact that Winchester has produced hardly any great men, replied, 'No, indeed, I should think not. We would pretty soon have knocked that out of them.' And the epigrams of the English temper usually take the form of understatement. 'Give Dayrolles a chair' were the last dying words of Lord Chesterfield, spoken of the friend who had come to see him. When the French troops go over the parapet to make an advance, their battle cry shouts the praises of their country. The British troops prefer to celebrate the advance in a more trivial fashion, 'This way to the early door, sixpence extra.'

I might go on interminably with this dissertation, but I have said enough for my purpose. The history of England has had much to do with moulding the English temper. We have been protected from direct exposure to the storms that have swept the Continent. Our wars on land have been adventures undertaken by expeditionary forces. At sea, while the power of England was growing, we have been explorers, pirates, buccaneers. Now that we are involved in a great European war on land, our methods have been changed. The artillery and infantry of a modern army cannot act effectively on their own impulse. We hold the sea, and the pirates' work for the present has passed into other hands. But our spirit and temper is the same as of old. It has found a new world in the air. War in the air, under the conditions of to-day, demands all the old gallantry and initiative. The airman depends on his own brain and nerve ; he cannot fall back on orders from his superiors. Our airmen of to-day are the true inheritors of Drake ; they have the same inspired recklessness, the same coolness, and the same chivalry to a vanquished enemy.

I am a very bad example of the English temper; for the English temper grumbles at all this, to the great relief of our enemies, who believe that what a man admits against his own nation must be true. Our pessimists, by indulging their natural vein, serve us, without reward, quite as well as Germany is served by her wireless press. They deceive the enemy.

Modern Germany has organized and regimented her people like an ant-hill or a beehive. The people themselves, including many who belong to the upper class, are often simple villagers in temper, full of kindness and anger, much subject to envy and jealousy, not magnanimous, docile and obedient to a fault. If they claimed, as individuals, to represent the highest reach

of European civilization, the claim would be merely
absurd.   So they shift their ground, and pretend that
society is greater than man, and that by their pains-
taking organization their society has been raised to the
pinnacle of human greatness.   They make this claim so
insistently, and in such obvious good faith, that some
few weak tempers and foolish minds in England have
been impressed by it.   These panic-stricken counsellors
advise us, without delay, to reform our institutions and
organize them upon the German model.   Only thus,
they tell us, can we hold our own against so huge
a power.   But if we were to take their advice, we
should have nothing of our own left to hold.   It is
reasonable and good to co-operate and organize in order
to attain an agreed object, but German organization
goes far beyond this.   The German nation is a carefully
built, smooth-running machine, with powerful engines.
It has only one fault--that any fool can drive it; and
seeing that the governing class in Germany is obstinate
and unimaginative, there is no lack of drivers to pilot
it to disaster.   The best ability of Germany is seen in
her military organization.   Napoleon is her worshipped
model, and, like many admirers of Napoleon, she thinks
only of his great campaigns ; she forgets that he died
in St. Helena, and that his schemes for the reorganiza-
tion of Europe failed.

   I know that many people in England are not daunted
but depressed by the military successes of the enemy.
Our soldiers in the field are not depressed.   But we
who are kept at home suffer from the miasma of the
back-parlour.   We read the headlines of newspapers—
a form of literature that is exciting enough, but does

not merit the praise given to Sophocles, who saw life steadily and saw it whole. We keep our ears to the telephone, and we forget that the great causes which are always at work, and which will shape the issues of this war, are not recorded upon the telephone. There are things truer and more important than the latest dispatches. Here is one of them. The organization of the second-rate can never produce anything first-rate. We do not understand a people who, when it comes to the last push of man against man, throw up their hands and utter the pathetic cry of 'Kamerad'. To surrender is a weakness that no one who has not been under modern artillery fire has any right to condemn; to profess a sudden affection for the advancing enemy is not weakness but baseness. Or rather, it would be baseness in a voluntary soldier; in the Germans it means only that the war is not their own war; that they are fighting as slaves, not as free men. The idea that we could ever live under the rule of these people is merely comic. To do them justice, they do not now entertain the idea, though they have dallied with it in the past.

No harm can be done, I think, by preaching to the English people the necessity for organization and discipline. We shall still be ourselves, and there is no danger that we shall overdo discipline or make organization a thing to be worshipped for its own sake. The danger is all the other way. We have learnt much from the war, and the work that we shall have to do when it ends is almost more important than the terms of peace, or concessions made this way and that. If the treacherous assault of the Germans on the liberties

and peace of Europe is rewarded by any solid gain to
the German Empire, then history may forgive them,
but this people of the British Empire will not forgive
them.   Nothing will be as it was before ; and our
cause, which will not be lost in the war, will still have
to be won in the so-called peace.   I know that some
say, ' Let us have war when we are at war, and peace
when we are at peace '.   It sounds plausible and magnanimous, but it is Utopian.   You must reckon with
your own people.   They know that when we last had
peace, the sunshine of that peace was used by the
Germans to hatch the spawn of malice and treason.   If
the Germans are defeated in the war, we shall, I suppose, forgive them, for the very English reason that it
is a bore not to forgive your enemies.   But if they
escape without decisive defeat in battle, their harder
trial is yet to come.

In some ways we are stronger than we have been
in all our long history.   We have found ourselves,
and we have found our friends.   Our dead have taught
the children of to-day more and better than any living
teachers can teach them.   No one in this country will
ever forget how the people of the Dominions, at the
first note of war, sprang to arms like one man.   We
must not thank or praise them ; like the Navy, they
regard our thanks and praise as something of an imper-
tinence.   They are not fighting, they say, for us.   But
that is how we discovered them.   They are doing much
better than fighting for us, they are fighting with us,
because, without a word of explanation or appeal, their
ideas and ours are the same.   We never have discussed
with them, and we never shall discuss, what is decent

and clean and honourable in human behaviour. A philosopher who is interested in this question can find plenty of intellectual exercise by discussing it with the Germans. Where an Englishman, a Canadian, and an Australian are met, there is no material for such a debate.

It would be extravagant to suppose that a discovery like this can leave our future relations untouched. We now know that we are profoundly united in a union much stronger and deeper than any mechanism can produce. I know how difficult a problem it is to hit on the best device for giving political expression to this union between States separated from one another by the whole world's diameter, differing in their circumstances, their needs, and their outlook. I do not dare to prescribe; but I should like to make a few remarks, and to call attention to a few points which are perhaps more present to the mind of the ordinary citizen than they are in the discussions of constitutional experts.

We must arrange for co-operation and mutual support. If the arrangement is complicated and lengthy, we must not wait for it; we must meet and discuss our common affairs. Ministers from the Dominions have already sat with the British Cabinet. We can never go back on that; it is a landmark in our history. Our Ministers must travel; if their supporters are impatient of their absence on the affairs of the Empire, they must find some less parochial set of supporters. We have begun in the right way; the right way is not to pass laws determining what you are to do; but to do what is needful, and do it at once,—do a lot of things, and regularize your successes by later legislation. Now is the time, while the Empire is white-hot.

Our first need is not lawyers, but men who, feeling
friendly, know how to behave as friends do. They
will not be impeached if they go beyond the letter of
the law. One act of faith is worth a hundred arguments. This is a family affair; the habits of an
affectionate and united family are the only good
model.

As for the Crown Colonies and India, the Dominions
must share our burden. It is objected, both here and
in India, that life in the Dominions is a very inadequate
education for the sympathetic handling of alien races
and customs. So is life in many parts of this island.
The fact is that the process of learning to govern these
alien peoples is the best education in the world. The
Indian Civil Service is a great College, and it governs
India. I can speak to this point, for I have lived
there and seen it at work. If India were really
governed by the ideas of the young novices who go
out there fresh from their examinations, she would
be a distressful country. But the novice is taken in
hand at once by the older members of the service;
he works under the eye of the Collector and the
Assistant Collector; they shoulder him and instruct
him as tame elephants shoulder and instruct the wild;
they are kind to him, and he lives in their company
while his prejudices and follies peel off him; so that
within a few years he becomes a tolerant, wise, and
devoted civil servant, who speaks the language of the
College and is proud to belong to it. The success of
the Government of India is not to be credited to the
classes from which the Civil Service is recruited, but
to the discipline of the Service itself, a Service so high

in tradition and so free from corruption that advancement in it is to be gained only by intelligence and sympathy. What I am saying is that I can imagine no finer raw material for the political discipline of the Indian Civil Service than some of the generous and clean-run spirits who have come from the Dominions to help in this war. They could be introduced to a share of our responsibilities without impeding or retarding the movement to give to selected natives of India a larger share in the government of their country.

But the war is not over, so I return to the main issue—the conflict between the English idea and the German idea of world government. It is not an accident, as Baron von Hügel remarks in his book on *The German Soul*, that the chief colonizing nation of the world should be a nation without a national army. We have depended enormously in the past on the initiative and virtue of the individual adventurer; if our adventurers were to fail us, which is not likely, or if the State were to supersede them, and attempt to do their work, which is not conceivable, our political power and influence would vanish with them. The world might perhaps be well ordered, but there would be no freedom, and no fun. The beauty of the adventurer is that he is practically invincible. He does not wait for orders. Under the most perfect police system that Germany could devise, he would be up and at it again. We are not so numerous as the Germans, but there are enough and to spare of us to make German government impossible in any place where we pitch our tents. We are practised hands at upsetting governments. Our political system is a training school for rebels. This is what makes our very existence an offence to the moral instincts of the German people. They are quite right to want to kill us; the only way to abolish fun and freedom is to abolish life. But I must not be unjust to them; their forethought provides for everything, and no doubt they would prescribe authorized forms of fun for half an hour a week, and would gather together their subjects in public assembly, under municipal regulations, to perform approved exercises in freedom.

Mankind lives by ideas; and if an irreconcilable difference in ideas makes a good war, then this is a good war. The contrast between the two ideas is profound and far-reaching. My business lies in a University. For a good many years before the war certain selected German students, who had had a University education in their own country, came as Rhodes scholars to Oxford. The intention of Mr. Rhodes was benevolent; he thought that if German students were to reside for four years at Oxford and to associate there, at an impressionable time of life, with young Englishmen, understanding and fellowship would be encouraged between the two peoples. But the German government took care to defeat Mr. Rhodes's intention. Instead of sending a small number of students for the full period, as Mr. Rhodes had provided, Germany asked and (by whose mistake I do not know) obtained leave to send a larger number for a shorter stay. The students selected were intended for the political and diplomatic service, and were older than the usual run of Oxford freshmen. Their behaviour had a certain ambassadorial flavour about it. They did not mix much in the many undergraduate societies which flourish in a college, but met together in clubs of their own to drink patriotic toasts. They were nothing if not superior. I remember a conversation I had with one of them who came to consult me. He wished, he said, to do some definite piece of research work in English literature. I asked him what problems or questions in English literature most interested him, and he replied that he would do anything that I advised. We had a talk of some length, wholly at cross-purposes. At last I tried to make my point of view clear by reminding him that research means finding the answer to a question, and that if his reading of English literature, which had been fairly extensive, had suggested no questions to his mind, he was not in the happiest possible position to begin research. This touched his national pride, and he gave me something not unlike a lecture. In Germany, he said, the professor tells you what you are to do; he gives you a subject for investigation, he names the books you are to read, and advises you on what you are to write; you follow his advice, and. produce a thesis, which gains you the degree of Doctor of Letters. I have seen a good many of these theses, and I am sure this account is correct. With very rare exceptions they are as dead as mutton, and much less nourishing. The upshot of our conversation was that he thought me an incompetent professor, and I thought him an unprofitable student.

There are many people in England to-day who praise the thoroughness of the Germans, and their devotion

to systematic thought. Has any one ever taken the
trouble to trace the development of the thesis habit,
and its influence on their national life? They theorize
everything, and they believe in their theories. They
have solemn theories of the English character, of the
French character, of the nature of war, of the history
of the world. No breath of scepticism dims their
complacency, although events steadily prove their
theories wrong. They have courage, and when they
are seeking truth by the process of reasoning, they
accept the conclusions attained by the process, however
monstrous these conclusions may be. They not only
accept them, they act upon them, and, as every one
knows, their behaviour in Belgium was dictated to
them by their philosophy.

Thought of this kind is the enemy of the human
race. It intoxicates sluggish minds, to whom thought
is not natural. It suppresses all the gentler instincts
of the heart and supplies a basis of orthodoxy for all
the cruelty and treachery in the world. I do not
know, none of us knows, when or how this war will
end. But I know that it is worth fighting to the end,
whatever it may cost to all and each of us. We may
have peace with the Germans, the peace of exhaustion
or the peace that is only a breathing space in a long
struggle. We can never have peace with the German
idea. It was not the idea of the older German thinkers
—of Kant, or of Goethe, who were good Europeans.
Kant said that there is nothing good in the world
except the good will. The modern German doctrine
is that there is nothing good in the world except what
tends to the power and glory of the State. The in-

ventor of this doctrine, it may be remembered, was the Devil, who offered to the Son of Man the glory of all the kingdoms of the world, if only He would fall down and worship him. The Germans, exposed to a like temptation, have accepted the offer and have fulfilled the condition. They can have no assurance that faith will be kept with them. On the other hand, we can have no assurance that they will suffer any signal or dramatic reverse. Human history does not usually observe the laws of melodrama. But we know that their newly purchased doctrine can be fought, in war and in peace, and we know that in the end it will not prevail.

THE FAITH OF ENGLAND

An Address to the Union Society of University College, London, March 22, 1917

WHEN Professor W. P. Ker asked me to address you on this ceremonial occasion I felt none of the confidence of the man who knows what he wants to say, and is looking for an audience. But Professor Ker is my old friend, and this place is the place where I picked up many of those fragmentary impressions which I suppose must be called my education. So I thought it would be ungrateful to refuse, even though it should prove that I have nothing to express save goodwill and the affections of memory.

When I matriculated in the University of London and became a student in this place, my professors were Professor Goodwin, Professor Church, Professor Henrici, Professor Croom Robertson, and Professor Henry Morley. I remember all these, though, if they were alive, I do not think that any of them would remember me. The indescribable exhilaration, which must be familiar to many of you, of leaving school and entering college, is in great part the exhilaration of making acquaintance with teachers who care much about their subject and little or nothing about their pupils. To escape from the eternal personal judgements which make a school a place of torment is to walk upon air. The schoolmaster looks at you; the college professor looks the way you are looking. The statements made by Euclid, that thoughtful Greek, are no longer encumbered at college with all those preposterous and irrelevant moral considerations which desolate the atmosphere of a school. The question now is not whether you have perfectly acquainted yourself with what Euclid said, but whether what he said is true. In my earliest days at college I heard a complete exposition of the first six books of Euclid, given in four lectures, with masterly ease and freedom, by Professor Henrici, who did not hesitate to employ methods of demonstration which, though they are perfectly legitimate and convincing, were rejected by the daintiness of the Greek. Professor Croom Robertson introduced his pupils to the mysteries of mental and moral philosophy, and incidentally disaffected some of us by what seemed to us his excessive reverence for the works of Alexander Bain. Those works were our favourite theme for satirical verse, which we did not pain our Professor by publishing. Professor Henry Morley lectured hour after hour to successive classes in a room half way down the passage, on the left. Even overwork could not deaden his enormous vitality; but I hope that his immediate successor does not lecture so often. Outside the classrooms I remember the passages, which resembled the cellars of an unsuccessful sculptor, the library, where I first read *Romeo and Juliet*, and the refectory, where we discussed human life in most, if not in all, of its aspects. In the neighbourhood of the College there was the classic severity of Gower Street, and, for those who preferred the richer variety of romance, there was always the Tottenham Court Road. Beyond all, and throughout all, there was friendship, and there was freedom. The College was founded, I believe, partly in the interests of those who object to subscribe to a conclusion before they are permitted to examine the grounds for it. It has always been a free place; and if I remember it as a place of delight, that is because I found here the delights of freedom.

My thoughts in these days are never very long away from the War, so that I should feel it difficult to speak of anything else. Yet there are so many ways in which it would be unprofitable for me to pretend to speak of it, that the difficulty remains. I have no knowledge of military or naval strategy. I am not intimately acquainted with Germany or with German culture. I could praise our own people, and our own fighting men, from a full heart; but that, I think, is not exactly what you want from me. So I am reduced to attempting what we have all had to attempt during the past two years or more, to try to state, for myself as much as for you, the meaning of this War so far as we can perceive it.

It seems to be a decree of fate that this country shall be compelled every hundred years to fight for her very life. We live in an island that lies across the mouths of the Rhine, and guards the access to all the ports of northern Europe. In this island we have had enough safety and enough leisure to develop for ourselves a system of constitutional and individual liberty which has had an enormous influence on other nations. It has been admired and imitated; it has also been hated and attacked. To the majority of European statesmen and politicians it has been merely unintelligible. Some of them have regarded it with a kind of superstitious reverence; for we have been very successful in the world at large, and how could so foolish and ineffective a system achieve success except by adventitious aid? Others, including all the statesmen and political theorists who prepared Germany for this War, have refused to admire; the power of England, they have taught, is not real power; she has been crafty and lucky; she has kept herself free from the entanglements and strifes of the Continent, and has enriched herself by filching the property of the combatants. If once she were compelled to hold by force what she won by guile, her pretensions would collapse, and she would fall back into her natural position as a small agricultural island, inhabited by a people whose proudest boast would then be that they are poor cousins of the Germans.

It is difficult to discuss this question with German professors and politicians: they have such simple minds, and they talk like angry children. Their opinions concerning England are not original; their views were held with equal fervour and expressed in very similar language by Philip of Spain in the sixteenth century, by Louis XIV of France in the seventeenth century, and by Napoleon at the close of the eighteenth century. 'These all died in faith, not having received the promises, but having seen them afar off.' I will ask you to consider the attack made upon England by each of these three powerful rulers.

Any one who reads the history of these three great wars will feel a sense of illusion, as if he were read-

ing the history of to-day. The points of resemblance
in all four wars are so many and so great that it seems
as if the four wars were all one war, repeated every
century. The cause of the war is always an ambitious
ruler who covets supremacy on the European Continent. England is always opposed to him—inevitably
and instinctively. It took the Germans twenty years
to prepare their people for this War. It took us two
days to prepare ours. Our instinct is quick and
sound ; for the resources and wealth of the Continent,
if once they were controlled by a single autocratic
power, would make it impossible for England to follow
her fortunes upon the sea. But we never stand quite
alone. The smaller peoples of the Continent, who
desire self-government, or have achieved it, always
give the conqueror trouble, and rebel against him or
resist him. England always sends help to them, the
help of an expeditionary force, or, failing that, the
help of irregular volunteers. Sir Philip Sidney dies
at Zutphen ; Sir John Moore at Corunna. There is
always desperate fighting in the Low Countries ; and
the names of Mons, Liège, Namur, and Lille recur
again and again. England always succeeds in maintaining herself, though not without some reverses, on
the sea. In the end the power of the master of legions,
Philip, Louis, Napoleon, and shall we say William,
crumbles and melts ; his ambitions are too costly to
endure, his people chafe under his lash, and his king-
dom falls into insignificance or is transformed by
internal revolution.

In all these wars there is one other resemblance
which it is good to remember to-day. The position

of England, at one time or another in the course of
the war, always seems desperate. When Philip of
Spain invaded England with the greatest navy of the
world, he was met on the seas by a fleet made up
chiefly of volunteers. When Louis overshadowed
Europe and threatened England, our king was in his
pay and had made a secret treaty with him; our
statesmen, moreover, had destroyed our alliance with
the maritime powers of Sweden and Holland, we had
war with the Dutch, and our fleet was beaten by them.
During the war against Napoleon we were in an even
worse plight; the plausible political doctrines of the
Revolution found many sympathizers in this country;
our sailors mutinied at the Nore; Ireland was aflame
with discontent; and we were involved in the Mah-
ratta War in India, not to mention the naval war
with America. Even after Trafalgar, our European
allies failed us, Napoleon disposed of Austria and
Prussia, and concluded a separate treaty with Russia.
It was then that Wordsworth wrote—

> ' 'Tis well! from this day forward we shall know
> That in ourselves our safety must be sought;
> That by our own right hands it must be wrought;
> That we must stand unpropped, or be laid low.
> O dastard whom such foretaste doth not cheer!
> We shall exult, if they who rule the land
> Be men who hold its many blessings dear,
> Wise, upright, valiant; not a servile band,
> Who are to judge of dangers which they fear,
> And honour which they do not understand.'

Always in the same cause, we have suffered worse
things than we are suffering to-day, and if there is
worse to come we hope that we are ready. The youngest

and best of us, who carry on and go through with it,
though many of them are dead and many more will
not live to see the day of victory, have been easily
the happiest and most confident among us. They
have believed that, at a price, they can save decency
and civilization in Europe, and, if they are wrong,
they have known, as we know, that the day when
decency and civilization are trampled under the foot
of the brute is a day when it is good to die.

When I speak of the German nation as the brute
I am not speaking controversially or rhetorically; the
whole German nation has given its hearty assent to
a brutal doctrine of war and politics; no facts need be
disputed between us: what to us is their shame, to
them is their glory. This is a grave difference; yet it
would be wrong to suppose that we can treat it ade-
quately by condemning the whole German nation as
a nation of confessed criminals. It is the paradox of
war that there is always right on both sides. When
a man is ready and willing to sacrifice his life, you
cannot deny him the right to choose what he will die
for. The most beautiful virtues, faith and courage
and devotion, grow like weeds upon the battle-field.
The fighters recognize these virtues in each other, and
the front lines, for all their mud and slaughter, are
breathed on by the airs of heaven. Hate and pusilla-
nimity have little there to nourish them. To find the
meaner passions you must seek further back. Johnson,
speaking in the *Idler* of the calamities produced by
war, admits that he does not know ' whether more is
to be dreaded from streets filled with soldiers accustomed to plunder, or from garrets filled with scribblers

accustomed to lie '. Now that our army is the nation
in arms, the danger from a lawless soldiery has become less, or has vanished ; but the other danger has
increased. Journalists are not the only offenders. It
is a strange, squalid background for the nobility of the
soldier that is made by the deceits and boasts of diplo-
matists and statesmen. In one of the prison camps of
England, some weeks ago, I saw a Saxon boy who had
fought bravely for his country. Simplicity and open-
ness and loyalty were written on his face. There are
hundreds like him, and I would not mention him
if it were not that that same day I read with a
new and heightened sense of disgust a speech by the
German Chancellor, writhing with timidity and dis-
honesty and uneasy braggadocio. Those who feel
this contrast as I did may be excused, I think, if they
come to the conclusion that to talk about war is an
accursed trade, and that to fight well, whether on the
one side or the other, is the only noble part.

Yet there is no escape for us; if we are to avoid
chaos, if the daily life of the world is to be re-estab-
lished and carried on, there must be an understanding
between nations, and there is no possible way to come
to an understanding save by the action and words of
representative men on the one side and the other. Such
representative men there are; there is no reason to
doubt that they do in the main truly express the
aspirations and wishes of their people, and on both
sides they have either explicitly or virtually made
offers. The offer of the Allied Powers is on record.
What does Germany offer ? She has refused to make
a definite statement, but her rulers have talked a

great deal, and what she intends is not really in doubt;
only she is not sure whether she can get it, and still
clings to the hope that a favourable turn of events
may relieve her of the duty of making proposals, and
put her in a position to dictate a settlement. We all
know what that settlement would be.

The German offer for a solution of the problem of
world-government is German sentiments, German
racial pride, German manners and customs, an immense
increase of German territory and German influence,
and above all an acknowledged supremacy for the
German race among the nations of the world. She
thinks she has not stated these aims in so many
words; but she has. When it was suggested that
the future peace of the world might be assured by
the formation of a League to Enforce Peace, Germany,
through her official spokesmen, expressed her sympathy with that idea, and stated that she would very
gladly put herself at the head of such a League.
I can hardly help loving the Germans when their
rustic simplicity and rustic cunning lead them all
unconsciously into self-revelation. The very idea of
a League to Enforce Peace implies equality among
the contracting parties; and Germany does not understand equality. 'By all means', she says, 'let us sit
at a round table, and I. will sit at the top of it.'
Her panacea for human ills is Germanism. She has
nothing to offer but a purely national sentiment,
which some, greatly privileged, may share, and the
rest must revere and bow to. In the Book of Genesis
we are told how Joseph was thrown into a pit by his
elder brothers for talking just like this; but he meant

it quite innocently, and so do the Germans. They do not intend irreverence to God when they call Him the good German God. On the contrary, they choose for His praise a word that to them stands for all goodness and all greatness. Their worship expresses itself naturally in the tribal ritual and the tribal creed. This tribal creed, there can be no doubt, is what they offer us for a talisman to ensure the right ordering of the world.

Patriotism and loyalty to hearth and home are passions so strong in humanity that a creed like this, when men are under its influence, is not easily seen to be absurd. The Saxon boy, whom I saw in his prison camp, probably would not quarrel with it. And even in the wider world of thought the illusions of nationalism are all-pervading. I once heard Professor Henry Sidgwick remark that it is not easy for us to understand how the troops of Portugal are stirred to heroic effort when their commanders call on them to remember that they are Portuguese. He would no doubt have been the first to admit, for he had an alert and sceptical mind, that it is only our stupidity which finds anything comic in such an appeal. But it is stupidity of this kind which unfits men to deal with other races, and it is stupidity of this kind which has been exalted by the Germans as a primal duty, and has, indeed, been advanced by them as their principal claim to undertake the government of the world.

This extreme nationalism, this unwillingness to feel any sympathy for other peoples, or to show them any consideration, has stupefied and blinded the Germans.

One of the heaviest charges that can be brought against them is that they have seen no virtue in France. I do not ask that they shall interrupt the War to express admiration for their enemies: I am speaking of the time before the War. France is the chief modern inheritor of that great Roman civilization which found us painted savages, and made us into citizens of the world. The French mind, it is admitted, and admitted most readily by the most intelligent men, is quick and delicate and perceptive, surer and clearer in its operation than the average European mind. Yet the Germans, infatuated with a belief in their own numbers and their own brute strength, have dared to express contempt for the genius of France. A contempt for foreigners is common enough among the vulgar and unthinking of all nations, but I do not believe that you will find anywhere but in Germany a large number of men trained in the learned professions who are so besotted by vanity as to deny to France her place in the vanguard of civilization. These louts cannot be informed or argued with; they are interested in no one but themselves, and naked self-assertion is their only idea of political argument. Treitschke, who was for twenty years Professor of History at Berlin, and, who did perhaps more than any other man to build up the modern German creed, has crystallized German politics in a single sentence. 'War', he says, 'is politics *par excellence,*' that is to say, politics at their purest and highest. Our political doctrine, if it must be put in as brief a form, would be better expressed in the sentence, 'War is the failure of politics'.

If England were given over to nationalism as
Germany is given over, then a war between these
two Powers, though it would still be a great dramatic
spectacle, would have as little meaning as a duel
between two rival gamebirds in a cockpit.　We
know, and it will some day dawn on the Germans,
that this War has a deeper meaning than that.　We
are not nationalist; we are too deeply experienced
in politics to stumble into that trap.　We have had
a better and longer political education than has come
to Germany in her short and feverish national life.
It is often said that the Germans are better educated
than we are, and in a sense that is true; they are
better furnished with schools and colleges and the
public means of education.　The best boy in a school
is the boy who best minds his book, and even if he
dutifully believes all that it tells him, that will not
lose him the prize.　When he leaves school and
graduates in a wider world, where men must depend
on their own judgement and their own energy, he is
often a little disconcerted to find that some of his less
bookish fellows easily outgo him in quickness of
understanding and resource.　German education is
too elaborate; it attempts to do for its pupils much
that they had better be left to do for themselves.
The pupils are docile and obedient, not troubled with
unruly doubts and questionings, so that the German
system of public education is a system of public
mesmerism, and, now that we see it in its effects,
may be truly described as a national disease.

I have said that England is not nationalist.　If the
English believed in England as the Germans believe

in Germany, there would be nothing for it but a duel to the death, the extinction of one people or the other, and darkness as the burier of the dead. Peace would be attained by a great simplification and impoverishment of the world. But the English do not believe in themselves in that mad-bull fashion. They come of mixed blood, and have been accustomed for many long centuries to settle their differences by compromise and mutual accommodation. They do not inquire too curiously into a man's descent if he shares their ideas. They have shown again and again that they prefer a tolerant and intelligent foreigner to rule over them rather than an obstinate and wrong-headed man of native origin. The earliest strong union of the various parts of England was achieved by William the Norman, a man of French and Scandinavian descent. Our native-born king, Charles the First, was put to death by his people; his son, James the Second, was banished, and the Dutchman, William the Third, who had proved himself a statesman and soldier of genius in his opposition to Louis the Fourteenth, was elected to the throne of England. The fierce struggles of the seventeenth century, between Royalists and Parliamentarians, between Cavaliers and Puritans, were settled at last, not by the destruction of either party, but by the stereotyping of the dispute in the milder and more tolerable shape of the party system. The only people we have ever shown ourselves unwilling to tolerate are the people who will tolerate no one but their own kind. We hate all Acts of Uniformity with a deadly hatred. We are careful for the rights of minorities. We think life should be made possible, and we do not object to its being made happy, for dissenters. Voltaire, the acutest French mind of his age, remarked on this when he visited England in 1726. 'England', he says, 'is the country of sects. "In my father's house are many mansions".... Although the Episcopalians and the Presbyterians are the two dominant sects in Great Britain, all the others are welcomed there, and live together very fairly, whilst most of the preachers hate one another almost as cordially as a Jansenist damns a Jesuit. Enter the London Exchange, a place much more worthy of respect than most Courts, and you see assembled for the benefit of mankind representatives of all nations. There the Jew, the Mohammedan, and the Christian deal with each other as if they were of the same religion, and call infidels only those who become bankrupt. There the Presbyterian trusts the Anabaptist, and the Anabaptist relies on the promise of the Quaker. On leaving these free and peaceful assemblies, some proceed to the synagogue, others to the tavern.... If in England there were only one religion, its despotism would be to be dreaded; if there were only two, their followers would cut each other's throats; but there are thirty of them, and they live in peace and happiness.'

Since we have had so much practice in tolerating one another, and in living together even when our ideas on life and the conduct of life seem absolutely incompatible, it is no wonder that we approach the treatment of international affairs in a temper very unlike the solemn and dogmatic ferocity of the German. We do not expect or desire that other peoples shall resemble us. The world is wide ; and the world-drama is enriched by multiplicity and diversity of character. We like bad men, if there is salt and spirit in their badness. We even admire a brute, if he is a whole-hearted brute. I have often thought that if the Germans had been true to their principles and their programme—if, after proclaiming that they meant to win by sheer strength and that they recognized no other right, they had continued as they began, and had battered and hacked, burned and killed, without fear or pity, a certain reluctant admiration for them might have been felt in this country. There is no chance of that now, since they took to whining about humanity. Yet it is very difficult wholly to alienate the sympathies of the English people. It is perhaps in some ways a weakness, as it is certainly in other ways a strength, that we are fanciers of other peoples. Our soldiers have a tendency to make pets of their prisoners, to cherish them as curiosities and souvenirs. The fancy becomes a passion when we find a little fellow struggling valiantly against odds. I suppose we should be at war with Germany to-day, even if the Germans had respected the neutrality of Belgium. But the unprovoked assault upon a little people that asked only to be let alone united all opinions in this country and brought us in with a rush. I believe there is one German, at least (I hope he is alive), who understands this. Early in July, 1914, a German student at Oxford, who was a friend and pupil of mine, came to say good-bye to me. I have since wondered whether he was under orders to join his regiment. Anyhow, we talked very freely of many

things, and he told me of an adventure that had be-
fallen him in an Oxford picture-palace. Portraits of
notabilities were being thrown on the screen. When
a portrait of the German Emperor appeared, a youth,
sitting just behind my friend, shouted out an insulting
and scurrilous remark. So my friend stood up and
turned round and, catching him a cuff on the head,
said, 'That's my emperor'. The house was full of
undergraduates, and he expected to be seized and
thrown into the street. To his great surprise the
undergraduates, many of whom have now fallen on
the fields of France, broke into rounds of cheering.
'I should like to think', my friend said, 'that a thing
like that could possibly happen in a German city, but
I am afraid that the feeling there would always be
against the foreigner. I admire the English; they
are so just.' I have heard nothing of him since,
except a rumour that he is with the German army of
occupation in Belgium. If so, I like to think of him
at a regimental mess, suggesting doubts, or, if that is
an impossible breach of military discipline, keeping
silence, when the loud-voiced major explains that the
sympathy of the English for Belgium is all pretence
and cant.

Ideal and disinterested motives are always to be
reckoned with in human nature. What the Germans
call 'real politics', that is to say, politics which treat
disinterested motives as negligible, have led them into
a morass and have bogged them there. How easy it
is to explain that the British Empire depends on trade,
that we are a nation of traders, that all our policy
is shaped by trade, that therefore it can only be

hypocrisy in us to pretend to any of the finer feelings.
This is not, as you might suppose, the harmless sally
of a one-eyed wit; it is the carefully reasoned belief
of Germany's profoundest political thinkers. They
do not understand a cavalier, so they confidently
assert that there is no such thing in nature. That is
a bad mistake to make about any nation, but perhaps
worst when it is made about the English, for the
cavalier temper in England runs through all classes.
You can find it in the schoolmaster, the small trader,
the clerk, and the labourer, as readily as in the officer
of dragoons, or the Arctic explorer. The Roundheads
won the Civil War, and bequeathed to us their
political achievements. From the Cavaliers we have
a more intimate bequest: it is from them, not from
the Puritans, that the fighting forces of the British
Empire inherit their outlook on the world, their
freedom from pedantry, and that gaiety and lightness
of courage which makes them carry their lives like
a feather in the cap.

I am not saying that our qualities, good or bad,
commend us very readily to strangers. The people of
England, on the whole, are respected more than they
are liked. When I call them fanciers of other nations,
I feel it only fair to add that some of those other
nations express the same truth in different language.
I have often heard the complaint made that Englishmen cannot speak of foreigners without an air of
patronage. It is impossible to deny this charge, for,
in a question of manners, the impressions you produce
are your manners; and there is no doubt about this
impression. There is a certain coldness about the

upright and humane Englishman which repels and
intimidates any trivial human being who approaches
him. Most men would forgo their claim to justice
for the chance of being liked. They would rather
have their heads broken, or accept a bribe, than be
the objects of a dispassionate judgement, however
kindly. They feel this so strongly that they experience a dull discomfort in any relationship that is not
tinctured with passion. As there are many such
relationships, not to be avoided even by the most
emotional natures, they escape from them by simulat-
ing lively feeling, and are sometimes exaggerated and
insincere in manner. They issue a very large paper
currency on a very small gold reserve. This, which
is commonly known as the Irish Question, is an in-
soluble problem, for it is a clash not of interests but
of temperaments. The English, it must in fairness be
admitted, do as they would be done by. No Englishman pure and simple is incommoded by the coldness
of strangers. He prefers it, for there are many stupid
little businesses in the world, which are falsified when
they are made much of; and even when important
facts are to be told, he would rather have them told
in a dreary manner. He hates a fuss.

The Germans, who are a highly emotional and
excitable people, have concentrated all their energy
on a few simple ideas. Their moral outlook is as
narrow as their geographical outlook is wide. Will
their faith prevail by its intensity, narrow and false
though it be? I cannot prove that it will not, but
I have a suspicion, which I think has already occurred
to some of them, that the world is too large and wilful

and strong to be mastered by them. We have seen what their hatchets and explosives can do, and they are nearing the end of their resources. They can still repeat some of their old exploits, but they make no headway, and time is not their friend.

One service, perhaps, they have done to civilization. There is a growing number of people who hold that when this War is over international relations must not be permitted to slip back into the unstable condition which tempted the Germans to their crime. A good many pacific theorists, no doubt, have not the experience and the imagination which would enable them to pass a useful judgement, or to make a valuable suggestion, on the affairs of nations. The abolition of war would be easily obtained if it were generally agreed that war is the worst thing that can befall a people. But this is not generally agreed; and, further, it is not true. While men are men they cannot be sure that they will never be challenged on a point of deep and intimate concern, where they would rather die than yield. But something can perhaps be done to discourage gamblers' wars, though even here any stockbroker will tell you how difficult it is to suppress gambling without injuring the spirit of enterprise. The only real check on war is an understanding between nations. For the strengthening of such an understanding the Allies have a great opportunity, and admirable instruments. I do not think that we shall call on Germany to preside at our conferences. But we shall have the help of all those qualities of heart and mind which are possessed by France, by Russia, by Italy, and by America, who, for all her caution, hates cruelty even more than she loves peace. There has never been an alliance of greater promise for the government and peace of the world.

What is the contribution of the British Empire, and of England, towards this settlement? Many of our domestic problems, as I have said, bear a curious resemblance to international problems. We have not solved them all. We have had many stumblings and many backslidings. But we have shown again and again that we believe in toleration on the widest possible basis, and that we are capable of generosity, which is a virtue much more commonly shown by private persons than by communities. We abolished the slave trade. We granted self-government to South Africa just after our war with her. Only a few days ago we gave India her will, and allowed her to impose a duty on our manufactures. Ireland could have self-government to-morrow if she did not value her feuds more than anything else in the world. All these are peoples to whom we have been bound by ties of kinship or trusteeship. A wider and greater opportunity is on its way to us. We are to see whether we are capable of generosity and trust towards peoples who are neither our kin nor our wards. Our understanding with France and Russia will call for great goodwill on both sides, not so much in the drafting of formal treaties as in indulging one another in our national habits. Families who fail to live together in unity commonly fail not because they quarrel about large interests, but because they do not like each other's little ways. The French are not a dull people; and the Russians are not a tedious people (what they do they do suddenly, without explanation); so that if we fail to take pleasure in them we have ourselves to blame. If we are not equal to our opportunities, if we do not learn to feel any affection for them, then not all the pacts and congresses in the world can make peace secure.

Of Germany it is too early to speak. We have not yet defeated her. If we do defeat her, no one who is acquainted with our temper and our record believes that we shall impose cruel or vindictive terms. If it were only the engineers of this war who were in question, we would destroy them gladly as common pests. But the thing is not so easy. A single home is in many ways a greater and more appealing thing than a nation; we should find ourselves thinking of the miseries of simple and ignorant people who have given their all for the country of their birth; and our hearts would fail us.

The Germans would certainly despise this address of mine, for I have talked only of morality, while they talk and think chiefly of machines. Zeppelins are a sad disappointment; but if any address on the War is being delivered to-night by a German professor, there can be no doubt that it deals with submarines, and treats them as the saviours of the Fatherland. Well, I know very little about submarines, but I notice that they have not had much success against ships of war. We are so easy-going that we expected to carry on our commerce in war very much as we did in peace. We have to change all that, and it will cost us not a little inconvenience, or even great hardships. But I cannot believe that a scheme of privy attacks on the traders of all nations, devised as a last resort, in lieu of naval victory, can be successful when it is no longer a surprise. And when I read history, I am strengthened in my belief that morality is all-important. I do not find that any war between great nations was ever won by a machine. The Trojan horse will be trotted out against me, but that was a municipal affair. Wars are won by the temper of a people. Serbia is not yet defeated. It is a frenzied and desperate quest that the Germans undertook when they began to seek for some mechanical trick or dodge, some monstrous engine, which should enable the less resolved and more excited people to defeat the more resolved and less excited. If we are to be defeated, it must be by them, not by their bogey-men. We got their measure on the Somme, and we found that when their guns failed to protect them, many of them threw up their hands. These men will never be our masters until we deserve to be their slaves.

So I am glad to be able to end on a note of agreement with the German military party. If they defeat us, it will be no more than we deserve. Till then, or till they throw up their hands, we shall fight them, and God will defend the right.

SOME GAINS OF THE WAR

An Address to the Royal Colonial Institute,
February 13, 1918

OUR losses in this War continue to be enormous, and we are not yet near to the end. So it may seem absurd to speak of our gains, of gains that we have already achieved. But if you will look at the thing in a large light, I think you will see that it is not absurd.

I do not speak of gains of territory, and prisoners, and booty. It is true that we have taken from the Germans about a million square miles of land in Africa, where land is cheap. We have taken more prisoners from them than they have taken from us, and we have whole parks of German artillery to set over against the battered and broken remnants of British field-guns which were exhibited in Berlin—a monument to the immortal valour of the little old Army. I am speaking rather of gains which cannot be counted as guns are counted, or measured as land is measured, but which are none the less real and important.

The Germans have achieved certain great material gains in this War, and they are fighting now to hold them. If they fail to hold them, the Germany of the war-lords is ruined. She will have to give up all her bloated ambitions, to purge and live cleanly, and painfully to reconstruct her prosperity on a quieter and sounder basis. She will not do this until she is forced to it by defeat. No doubt there are moderate and sensible men in Germany, as in other countries; but in

Germany they are without influence, and can do nothing. War is the national industry of Prussia; Prussia has knit together the several states of the larger Germany by means of war, and has promised them prosperity and power in the future, to be achieved by war. You know the Prussian doctrine of war. Every one now knows it. According to that doctrine it is a foolish thing for a nation to wait till it is attacked. It should carefully calculate its own strength and the strength of its neighbours, and, when it is ready, it should attack them, on any pretext, suddenly, without warning, and should take from them money and land. When it has gained territory in this fashion, it should subject the population of the conquered territory to the strictest laws of military service, and so supply itself with an instrument for new and bolder aggression. This is not only the German doctrine; it is the German practice. In this way and no other modern Germany has been built up. It is a huge new State, founded on force, cemented by fear, and financed on speculative gains to be derived from the great gamble of war. You may have noticed that the German people have not been called on, as yet, to pay any considerable sum in taxation towards the expenses of this war. Those expenses (that, at least, was the original idea) were to be borne wholly by the conquered enemy. There are hundreds of thousands of Germans to-day who firmly believe that their war-lords will return in triumph from the stricken field, bringing with them the spoils of war, and scattering a largess of peace and plenty.

To us it seems a marvel that any people should accept such a doctrine, and should willingly give their lives and their fortunes to the work of carrying it out in practice; but it is not so marvellous as it seems. The German peoples are brave and obedient, and so make good soldiers; they are easily lured by the hope of profit; they are naturally attracted by the spectacular and sentimental side of war; above all, they are so curiously stupid that many of them do actually believe that they are a divinely chosen race, superior to the other races of the world. They are very carefully educated, and their education, which is ordered by the State, is part of the military machine. Their thinking is done for them by officials. It would require an extraordinary degree of courage and independence for a German youth to cut himself loose and begin thinking and judging for himself. It must always be remembered, moreover, that their recent history seems to justify their creed. I will not go back to Frederick the Great, though the history of his wars is the Prussian handbook, which teaches all the characteristic Prussian methods of treachery and deceit. But consider only the last two German wars. How, in the face of these, can it be proved to any German that war is not the most profitable of adventures? In 1866 Prussia had war with Austria. The war lasted forty days, and Prussia had from five to six thousand soldiers killed in action. As a consequence of the war Prussia gained much territory, and established her control over the states of greater Germany. In 1870 she had war with France. Her total casualties in that war were approximately a hundred thousand, just about the same as our casualties in Gallipoli. From the war she gained, besides a great increase of strength at home, the rich provinces of Alsace and Lorraine, with all their mineral wealth, and an indemnity of two hundred million pounds, that is to say, four times the actual cost of the war in money. How then can it be maintained that war is not good business? If you say so to any Prussian, he thinks you are talking like a child.

Not only were these two wars rich in profit for the Germans, but they did not lose them much esteem. There was sympathy in this country for the union of the German peoples, just as there was sympathy, a few years earlier, for the union of the various states of Italy. There was not a little admiration for German efficiency and strength. So that Bismarck, who was an expert in all the uses of bullying, blackmail, and fraud, was accepted as a great European statesman. I have always believed, and I still believe, that Germany will have to pay a heavy price for Bismarck—all the heavier because the payment has been so long deferred.

The present War, then, is in the direct line of succession to these former wars; it was planned by Germany, elaborately and deliberately planned, on a calculation of the profits to be derived from operations on a large scale.

Well, as I said, we, as a people, do not believe in gambling in human misery to attain uncertain speculative gains. We hold that war can be justified only by a good cause, not by a lucky event. The German doctrine seems to us impious and wicked. Though we have defined our war aims in detail, and the Germans have not dared publicly to define theirs, our real and sufficient war aim is to break the monstrous and inhuman doctrine and practice of the enemy—to make their calculations miscarry. And observe, if their calculations miscarry, they have fought and suffered for nothing

They entered into this War for profit, and in the conduct of the War, though they have made many mistakes, they have made none of those generous and magnanimous mistakes which redeem and beautify a losing cause.

The essence of our cause, and its greatest strength, is that we are not fighting for profit. We are fighting for no privilege except the privilege of possessing our souls, of being ourselves—a privilege which we claim also for other weaker nations. The inestimable strength of that position is that if the odds are against us it does not matter. If you see a ruffian torturing a child, and interfere to prevent him, do you feel that your attempt was a wrong one because he knocks you down? And if you succeed, what material profit is there in saving a child from torture? We have sometimes fought in the past for doubtful causes and for wrong causes, but this time there is no mistake. Our cause is better than we deserve; we embraced it by an act of faith, and it is only by continuing in that faith that we shall see it through. The little old Army, when they went to France in August 1914, did not ask what profits were likely to come their way. They knew that there were none, but they were willing to sacrifice themselves to save decency and humanity from being trampled in the mud. This was the Army that the Germans called a mercenary Army, and its epitaph has been written by a good poet:

> These, in the day when heaven was falling,
> The hour when earth's foundations fled,
> Followed their mercenary calling,
> And took their wages, and are dead.

Their shoulders held the heavens suspended,
They stood, and earth's foundations stay,
What God abandoned these defended,
And saved the sum of things for pay.

We must follow their example, for we shall never get a better. We must not make too much of calculation, especially when it deals with incalculable things. Nervous public critics, like Mr. H. G. Wells, are always calling out for more cleverness in our methods, for new and effective tricks, so that we may win the War. I would never disparage cleverness ; the more you can get of it, the better ; but it is useless unless it is in the service of something stronger and greater than itself, and that is character. Cleverness can grasp ; it is only character that can hold. The Duke of Wellington was not a clever man ; he was a man of simple and honourable mind, with an infinite capacity for patience, persistence, and endurance, so that neither unexpected reverses abroad nor a flood of idle criticism at home could shake him or change him. So he bore a chief part in laying low the last great tyranny that desolated Europe.

None of our great wars was won by cleverness ; they were all won by resolution and perseverance. In all of them we were near to despair and did not despair. In all of them we won through to victory in the end.

But in none of them did victory come in the expected shape. The worst of making elaborate plans of victory, and programmes of all that is to follow victory, is that the mixed event is sure to defeat those plans. Not every war finds its decision in a single great battle. Think of our war with Spain in the sixteenth century. Spain was then the greatest of European Powers. She

had larger armies than we could raise; she had more
than our wealth, and more than our shipping. The
newly discovered continent of America was an appanage
of Spain, and her great galleons were wafted lazily to
and fro, bringing her all the treasures of the western
hemisphere. We defeated her by standing out and
holding on. We fought her in the Low Countries,
which she enslaved and oppressed. We refused to
recognize her exclusive rights in America, and our
merchant seamen kept the sea undaunted, as they have
kept it for the last three years. When at last we
became an intolerable vexation to Spain, she collected
a great Armada, or war-fleet, to invade and destroy us;
and it was shattered, by the winds of heaven and the
sailors of England, in 1588. The defeat of the Armada
was the turning-point of the war, but it was not the
end. It lifted a great shadow of fear from the hearts
of the people, as a great shadow of fear has already
been lifted from their hearts in the present War, but
during the years that followed we suffered many and
serious reverses at the hand of Spain, before peace and
security were reached. So late as 1601, thirteen years
after the defeat of the Armada, the King of Denmark
offered to mediate between England and Spain, so that
the long and disastrous war might be ended. Queen
Elizabeth was then old and frail, but this was what she
said—and if you want to understand why she was
almost adored by her people, listen to her words: 'I
would have the King of Denmark, and all Princes
Christian and Heathen to know, that England hath no
need to crave peace; nor myself endured one hour's
fear since I attained the crown thereof, being guarded

with so valiant and faithful subjects.' In the end the
power and menace of Spain faded away, and when
peace was made, in 1604, this nation never again, from
that day to this, feared the worst that Spain could do.

What were our gains from the war with Spain?
Freedom to live our lives in our own way, unthreatened;
freedom to colonize America. The gains of a great war
are never visible immediately; they are deferred, and
extended over many years. What did we gain by our
war with Napoleon, which ended in the victory of
Waterloo? For long years after Waterloo this country
was full of riots and discontents; there were rick-
burnings, agitations, popular risings, and something
very near to famine in the land. But all these things,
from a distance, are now seen to have been the broken
water that follows the passage of a great storm. The
real gains of Waterloo, and still more of Trafalgar, are
evident in the enormous commercial and industrial
development of England during the nineteenth century,
and in the peaceful foundation of the great dominions of
Canada, Australia, and South Africa, which was made
possible only by our unchallenged use of the seas. The
men who won those two great battles did not live to
gather the fruits of their victory; but their children
did. If we defeat Germany as completely as we hope,
we shall not be able to point at once to our gains. But
it is not a rash forecast to say that our children and
children's children will live in greater security and
freedom than we have ever tasted.

A man must have a good and wide imagination if he
is to be willing to face wounds and death for the sake
of his unborn descendants and kinsfolk. We cannot

count on the popular imagination being equal to the
task. Fortunately, there is a substitute for imagination
which does the work as well or better, and that is
character. Our people are sound in instinct; they
understand a fight. They know that a wrestler who
considers, while he is in the grip of his adversary,
whether he would not do well to give over, and so put
an end to the weariness and the strain, is no sort of
a wrestler. They have never failed under a strain of
this kind, and they will not fail now. The people who
do the half-hearted and timid talking are either young
egotists, who are angry at being deprived of their
personal ease and independence; or elderly pensive
gentlemen, in public offices and clubs, who are no
longer fit for action, and, being denied action, fall into
melancholy; or feverish journalists, who live on the
proceeds of excitement, who feel the pulse and take the
temperature of the War every morning, and then rush
into the street to announce their fluttering hopes and
fears; or cosmopolitan philosophers, to whom the change
from London to Berlin means nothing but a change in
diet and a pleasant addition to their opportunities of
hearing good music; or aliens in heart, to whom the
historic fame of England, 'dear for her reputation
through the world,' is less than nothing; or practical
jokers, who are calm and confident enough themselves,
but delight in startling and depressing others. These
are not the people of England; they are the parasites
of the people of England. The people of England
understand a fight.

That brings me to the first great gain of the War.
We have found ourselves. Which of us, in the early

months of 1914, would have dared to predict the splendours of the youth of this Empire—splendours which are now a part of our history? We are adepts at self-criticism and self-depreciation. We hate the language of emotion. Some of us, if we were taken to heaven and asked what we thought of it, would say that it is decent, or not so bad. I suppose we are jealous to keep our standard high, and to have something to say if a better place should be found. But in spite of all this, we do now know, and it is worth knowing, that we are not weaker than our fathers. We know that the people who inhabit these islands and this commonwealth of nations cannot be pushed on one side, or driven under, or denied a great share in the future ordering of the world. We know this, and our knowledge of it is the debt that we owe to our dead. It is not vanity to admit that we know it; on the contrary, it would be vanity to pretend that we do not know it. It is visible to other eyes than ours. Some time ago I heard an address given by a friend of mine, an Indian Mohammedan of warrior descent, to University students of his own faith. He was urging on them the futility of dreams and the necessity of self-discipline and self-devotion. 'Why do the people of this country', he said, 'count for so much all the world over? It is not because of their dreams; it is because thousands of them are lying at the bottom of the sea.'

Further, we have not only found ourselves; we have found one another. A new kindliness has grown up, during the War, between people divided by the barriers of class, or wealth, or circumstance. A statesman of the seventeenth century remarks that *It is a Misfortune*

for a Man not to have a Friend in the World, but for
that reason he shall have no Enemy. I might invert his
maxim and say, *It is a Misfortune for a Man to have*
many Enemies, but for that reason he shall know who
are his Friends. No Radical member of Parliament
will again, while any of us live, cast contempt on 'the
carpet Captains of Mayfair'. No idle Tory talker will
again dare to say that the working men of England
care nothing for their country. Even the manners of
railway travel have improved. I was travelling in a
third-class compartment of a crowded train the other
day ; we were twenty in the compartment, but it seemed
a pity to leave any one behind, and we made room for
number twenty-one. Nothing but a very kindly human
feeling could have packed us tight enough for this. Yet
now is the time that has been chosen by some of these
pensive gentlemen that I spoke of, and by some of these
excitable journalists, to threaten us with class-war, and
to try to make our flesh creep by conjuring up the horrors
of revolution. I advise them to take their opinions to
the third-class compartment and discuss them there. It
is a good tribunal, for, sooner or later, you will find
every one there—even officers, when they are travelling
in mufti at their own expense. I have visited this
tribunal very often, and I have always come away from
it with the same impression, that this people means
to win the War. But I do not travel much in the
North of England, so I asked a friend of mine, whose
dealings are with the industrial North, what the work-
people of Lancashire and Yorkshire think of the War.
He said, 'Their view is very simple : they mean to
win it ; and they mean to make as much money out

of it as ever they can.' Certainly, that is very simple; but before you judge them, put yourselves in their place. There are great outcries against profiteers, for making exorbitant profits out of the War, and against munition workers, for delaying work in order to get higher wages. I do not defend either of them; they are unimaginative and selfish, and I do not care how severely they are dealt with; but I do say that the majority of them are not wicked in intention. A good many of the more innocent profiteers are men whose sin is that they take an offer of two shillings rather than an offer of eighteenpence for what cost them one and a penny. Some of us, in our weaker moments, might be betrayed into doing the same. As for the munition workers, I remember what Goldsmith, who had known the bitterest poverty, wrote to his brother. 'Avarice', he said, 'in the lower orders of mankind is true ambition; avarice is the only ladder the poor can use to preferment. Preach then, my dear Sir, to your son, not the excellence of human nature nor the disrespect of riches, but endeavour to teach him thrift and economy. Let his poor wandering uncle's example be placed in his eyes. I had learned from books to love virtue before I was taught from experience the necessity of being selfish.'

The profiteers and the munition workers are endeavouring, incidentally, to better their own position. But make no mistake; the bulk of these people would rather die than allow one spire of English grass to be trodden under the foot of a foreign trespasser. Their chief sin is that they do not fear. They think that there is plenty of time to do a little business for themselves on the way to defeat the enemy. I cannot help remembering the mutiny at the Nore, which broke out in our fleet during the Napoleonic wars.   The mutineers struck for more pay and better treatment, but they agreed together that if the French fleet should put in an appearance during the mutiny, all their claims should be postponed for a time, and the French fleet should have their first attention.

Employers and employed do, no doubt, find in some trades to-day that their relations are strained and irksome. They would do well to take a lesson from the Army, where, with very few exceptions, there is harmony and understanding between those who take orders and those who give them.   It is only in the Army that you can see realized the ideal of ancient Rome.

> Then none was for a party,
>   Then all were for the State ;
> Then the great man helped the poor,
>   And the poor man loved the great.

Why is the Army so far superior to most commercial and industrial businesses ?   The secret does not lie in State employment.   There is plenty of discontent and unrest among the State-employed railway men and munition workers.   It lies rather in the habit of mutual help and mutual trust.   If any civilian employer of labour wants to have willing workpeople, let him take a hint from the Army.   Let him live with his work-people, and share all their dangers and discomforts. Let him take thought for their welfare before his own, and teach self-sacrifice by example.   Let him put the good of the nation before all private interests ; and those whom he commands will do for him anything that he asks.

I cannot believe that the benefits which have come to us from the Army will pass away with the passing of the War. Those who have been comrades in danger will surely take with them something of the old spirit into civil life. And those who have kept clear of the Army in order to carry on their own trades and businesses will surely realize that they have missed the great opportunity of their lives.

In a wider sense the War has brought us to an understanding of one another. This great Commonwealth of independent nations which is called the British Empire is scattered over the surface of the habitable globe. It embraces people who live ten thousand miles apart, and whose ways of life are so different that they might seem to have nothing in common. But the War has brought them together, and has done more than half a century of peace could do to promote a common understanding. Hundreds of thousands of men of our blood who, before the War, had never seen this little island, have now made acquaintance with it. Hundreds of thousands of the inhabitants of this island to whom the Dominions were strange, far places, if, after the War, they should be called on to settle there, will not feel that they are leaving home. I can only hope that the Canadians and Anzacs think as well of us as we do of them. We do not like to praise our friends in their hearing, so I will say no more than this : I am told that a new kind of peerage, very haughty and very self-important, has arisen in South London. Its members are those householders who have been privileged to have Anzac soldiers billeted on them. It is private ties of this

kind, invisible to the constitutional lawyer and the
political historian, which make the fine meshes of the
web of Empire.

Because he knew that the strength of the whole
texture depends on the strength of the fine meshes,
Earl Grey, who died last year, will always be remembered in our history. Not many men have his opportunity to make acquaintance with the domain that is
their birthright, for he had administered a province of
South Africa, and had been Governor-General of Canada.
He rediscovered the glory of the Empire, as poets redis-
cover the glory of common speech. ' He had breathed
its air,' a friend of his says, ' fished its rivers, walked in
its valleys, stood on its mountains, met its people face
to face. He had seen it in all the zones of the world.
He knew what it meant to mankind. Under the
British flag, wherever he journeyed, he found men of
English speech living in an atmosphere of liberty and
carrying on the dear domestic traditions of the British
Isles. He saw justice firmly planted there, industry and
invention hard at work unfettered by tyrants of any
kind, domestic life prospering in natural conditions, and
our old English kindness and cheerfulness and broad-
minded tolerance keeping things together. But he
also saw room under that same flag, ample room, for
millions and millions more of the human race. The
Empire wasn't a word to him. It was a vast, an almost
boundless, home for honest men.'

The War did not dishearten him. When he died,
in August, 1917, he said, ' Here I lie on my death-bed,
looking clear into the Promised Land. I'm not allowed
to enter it, but there it is before my eyes. After the

War the people of this country will enter it, and those who laughed at me for a dreamer will see that I wasn't so wrong after all. But there's still work to do for those who didn't laugh, hard work, and with much opposition in the way; all the same, it is work right up against the goal. My dreams have come true.'

One of the clear gains of the War is to be found in the increased activity and alertness of our own people. The motto of to-day is, 'Let those now work who never worked before, And those who always worked now work the more.' Before the War we had a great national reputation for idleness—in this island, at least. I remember a friendly critic from Canada who, some five or six years ago, expressed to me, with much disquiet, his opinion that there was something very far wrong with the old country; that we had gone soft. As for our German critics, they expressed the same view in gross and unmistakable fashion. Wit is not a native product in Germany, it all has to be imported, so they could not satirize us; but their caricatures of the typical Englishman showed us what they thought. He was a young weakling with a foolish face, and was dressed in cricketing flannels. It would have been worth their while to notice what they did not notice, that his muscles and nerves are not soft. They learned that later, when the bank-clerks of Manchester broke the Prussian Guard into fragments at Contalmaison. This must have been a sad surprise, for the Germans had always taught, in their delightful authoritative fashion, that the chief industries of the young Englishman are lawn-tennis and afternoon tea. They are a fussy people, and they find it difficult to understand the calm of the

man who, having nothing to do, does it. Perhaps they
were right, and we were too idle. The disease was
never so serious as they thought it, and now, thanks to
them, we are in a fair way to recovery. The idle classes
have turned their hand to the lathe and the plough.
Women are doing a hundred things that they never did
before, and are doing them well. The elasticity and
resourcefulness that the War has developed will not be
lost or destroyed by the coming of peace. Least of all
will those qualities be lost if we should prove unable,
in this War, to impose our own terms on Germany.
Then the peace that follows will be a long struggle, and
in that struggle we shall prevail. In the last long
peace we were not suspicious; we felt friendly enough
to the Germans, and we gave them every advantage.
They despised us for our friendliness and used the peace
to prepare our downfall. That will never happen again.
If we cannot tame the cunning animal that has assaulted
humanity, at least we can and will tether him. Laws
will not be necessary; there are millions of others
besides the seamen of England who will have no
dealings with an unsubdued and unrepentant Germany.
What the Germans are not taught by the War they
will have to learn in the more tedious and no less costly
school of peace.

In any case, whether we win through to real peace
and real security, or whether we are thrown back on an
armed peace and the duty of unbroken vigilance, we
shall be dependent for our future on the children
who are now learning in the schools or playing in
the streets. It is a good dependence. The children
of to-day are better than the children whom I knew

when I was a child.   I think they have more intelligence
and sympathy; they certainly have more public spirit.
We cannot do too much for them.   The most that we
can do is nothing to what they are going to do for us,
for their own nation and people.   I am not concerned
to discuss the education problem.   Formal education,
carried on chiefly by means of books, is a very small
part of the making of a man or a woman.   But I am
interested to know what the children are thinking.   You
cannot fathom a child's thoughts, but we know who are
their best teachers, and what lessons have been stamped
indelibly on their minds.   Their teachers, whom they
never saw, and whose lessons they will never forget, lie
in graves in Flanders and France and Gallipoli and
Syria and Mesopotamia, or unburied at the bottom of
the sea.   The runner falls, but the torch is carried
forward.   This is what Julian Grenfell, who gave his
mind and his life to the War, has said in his splendid
poem called *Into Battle*:

> And life is colour and warmth and light,
> And a striving evermore for these;
> And he is dead who will not fight,
> And who dies fighting hath increase.

Those who died fighting will have such increase that a
whole new generation, better even than the old, will be
ready, no long time hence, to uphold and extend and
decorate the Commonwealth of nations which their
fathers and brothers saved from ruin.

One thing I have never heard discussed, but it is the
clearest gain of all, and already it may be called a
certain gain.   After the War the English language will
have such a position as it has never had before.   It will

be established in world-wide security. Even before the
War, it may be truly said, our language was in no
danger from the competition of the German language.
The Germans have never had much success in the attempt
to get their language adopted by other peoples. Not
all the military laws of Prussia can drive out French
from the hearts and homes of the people of Alsace. In
the ports of the near and far East you will hear English
spoken—pidgin English, as it is called, that is to say, a
selection of English words suited for the business of
daily life. But you may roam the world over, and you
will hear no pidgin German. Before the War many
Germans learned English, while very few English-
speaking people learned German. In other matters we
disagreed, but we both knew which way the wind was
blowing. It may be said, and said truly, that our well-
known laziness was one cause of our failing or neglect-
ing to learn German. But it was not the only cause ;
and we are not lazy in tasks which we believe to be
worth our while. Rather we had an instinctive belief
that the future does not belong to the German tongue.
That belief is not likely to be impaired by the War.
Armed ruffians can do some things, but one thing they
cannot do ; they cannot endear their language to those
who have suffered from their violence. The Germans
poisoned the wells in South-West Africa ; in Europe
they did all they could to poison the wells of mutual
trust and mutual understanding among civilized men.
Do they think that these things will make a good
advertisement for the explosive guttural sounds and
the huddled deformed syntax of the speech in which
they express their arrogance and their hate? Which

of the chief European languages will come first, after the War, with the little nations? Will Serbia be content to speak German? Will Norway and Denmark feel a new affection for the speech of the men who have degraded the old humanity of the seas? Neighbourhood, kinship, and the necessities of commerce may retain for the German language a certain measure of custom in Sweden and Switzerland, and in Holland. But for the most part Germans will have to· be content to be addressed in their own tongue only by those who fear them, or by those who hope to cheat them.

This gain, which I make bold to predict for the English language, is a real gain, apart from all patriotic bias. The English language is incomparably richer, more fluid, and more vital than the German language. Where the German has but one way of saying a thing, we have two or three, each with its distinctions and its subtleties of usage. Our capital wealth is greater, and so are our powers of borrowing. English sprang from the old Teutonic stock, and we can still coin new words, such as 'food-hoard' and 'joy-ride', in the German fashion. But long centuries ago we added thousands of Romance words, words which came into English through the French or Norman-French, and brought with them the ideas of Latin civilization and of mediaeval Christianity. Later on, when the renewed study of Latin and Greek quickened the intellectual life of Europe, we imported thousands of Greek and Latin words direct from the ancient world, learned words, many of them, suitable for philosophers, or for writers who pride themselves on shooting a little above the vulgar apprehension. Yet many of these, too, have found their way into daily speech, so that we can say most things in three ways, according as we draw on one or another of the three main sources of our speech. Thus, you can Begin, or Commence, or Initiate an undertaking, with Boldness, or Courage, or Resolution. If you are a Workman, or Labourer, or Operative, you can Ask, or Request, or Solicit your employer to Yield, or Grant, or Concede, an increase in the Earnings, or Wages, or Remuneration which fall to the lot of your Fellow, or Companion, or Associate. Your employer is perhaps Old, or Veteran, or Superannuated, which may Hinder, or Delay, or Retard the success of your application. But if you Foretell, or Prophesy, or Predict that the War will have an End, or Close, or Termination that shall not only be Speedy, or Rapid, or Accelerated, but also Great, or Grand, or Magnificent, you may perhaps Stir, or Move, or Actuate him to have Ruth, or Pity, or Compassion on your Mate, or Colleague, or Collaborator.

The English language, then, is a language of great wealth—much greater wealth than can be illustrated by any brief example. But wealth is nothing unless you can use it. The real strength of English lies in the inspired freedom and variety of its syntax. There is no grammar of the English speech which is not comic in its stiffness and inadequacy. An English grammar does not explain all that we can do with our speech; it merely explains what shackles and restraints we must put upon our speech if we would bring it within the comprehension of a school-bred grammarian. But the speech itself is like the sea, and soon breaks down the dykes built by the inland engineer. It was the fashion, in the eighteenth century, to speak of the divine Shakespeare.

The reach and catholicity of his imagination was what earned him that extravagant praise ; but his syntax has no less title to be called divine.   It is not cast or wrought, like metal ; it leaps like fire, and moves like air.   So is every one that is born of the spirit.   Our speech is our great charter.   Far better than in the long constitutional process whereby we subjected our kings to law, and gave dignity and strength to our Commons, the meaning of English freedom is to be seen in the illimitable freedom of our English speech.

Our literature is almost as rich as our language. Modern German literature begins in the eighteenth century.   Modern English literature began with Chaucer, in the fourteenth century, and has been full of great names and great books ever since.   Nothing has been done in German literature for which we have not a counterpart, done as well or better—except the work of Heine, and Heine was a Jew.   His opinion of the Prussians was that they are a compost of beer, deceit, and sand.   French literature and English literature can be compared, throughout their long course, sometimes to the great advantage of the French.   German literature cannot seriously be compared with either.

It may be objected that literature and art are ornamental affairs, which count for little in the deadly strife of nations.   But that is not so.   Our language cannot go anywhere without taking our ideas and our creed with it, not to mention our institutions and our games. If the Germans could understand what Chaucer means when he says of his Knight that

he lovèd chivalry,
Truth and honoùr, freedom and courtesy,

then indeed we might be near to an understanding. I asked a good German scholar the other day what is the German word for 'fair play'. He replied, as they do in Parliament, that he must ask for notice of that question. I fear there is no German word for 'fair play'.

The little countries, the pawns and victims of German policy, understand our ideas better. The peoples who have suffered from tyranny and oppression look to England for help, and it is a generous weakness in us that we sometimes deceive them by our sympathy, for our power is limited, and we cannot help them all. But it will not count against us at the final reckoning that in most places where humanity has suffered cruelty and indignity the name of England has been invoked : not always in vain.

And now, for I have kept to the last what I believe to be the greatest gain of all, the entry of America into the War assures the triumph of our common language. America is peopled by many races ; only a minority of the inhabitants—an influential and governing minority— are of the English stock. But here, again, the language carries it ; and the ideas that inspire America are ideas which had their origin in the long English struggle for freedom. Our sufferings in this War are great, but they are not so great that we cannot recognize virtue in a new recruit to the cause. No nation, in the whole course of human history, has ever made a more splendid decision, or performed a more magnanimous act, than America, when she decided to enter this War. She had nothing to gain, for, to say the bare truth, she had little to lose. If Germany were to dominate the world, America, no doubt, would be ruined ; but in all human

likelihood, Germany's impious attempt would have spent
itself and been broken long before it reached the coasts
of America. America might have stood out of the
War in the assurance that her own interests were safe,
and that, when the tempest had passed, the centre of
civilization would be transferred from a broken and
exhausted Europe to a peaceful and prosperous America.
Some few Americans talked in this strain, and favoured
a decision in this sense. But it was not for nothing
that America was founded upon religion. When she
saw humanity in anguish, she did not pass by on the
other side. Her entry into the War has put an end, I
hope for ever, to the family quarrel, not very profound
or significant, which for a century and a half has been
a jarring note in the relations of mother and daughter.
And it has put an end to another danger. It seemed
at one time not unlikely that the English language as it
is spoken overseas would set up a life of its own, and
become separated from the language of the old country.
A development of this kind would be natural enough.
The Boers of South Africa speak Dutch, but not the
Dutch spoken in Holland. The French Canadians
speak French, but not the French of Molière. Half
a century ago, when America was exploring and settling
her own country, in wild and lone places, her pioneers
enriched the English speech with all kinds of new and
vivid phrases. The tendency was then for America to go
her own way, and to cultivate what is new in language
at the expense of what is old. She prided herself even
on having a spelling of her own, and seemed almost
willing to break loose from tradition and to coin a new
American English.

This has not happened; and now, I think, it will not happen. For one thing, the American colonists left us when already we had a great literature. Chaucer, Shakespeare, and Spenser belong to America no less than to us, and America has never forgotten them. The education which has been fostered in American schools and colleges keeps the whole nation in touch with the past. Some of their best authors write in a style that Milton and Burke would understand and approve. There is no more beautiful English prose than Nathaniel Hawthorne's. The best speeches of Abraham Lincoln, and, we may truly add, of President Wilson, are merely classic English. During my own lifetime I am sure I have seen the speech usages of the two peoples draw closer together. For one thing, we on this side now borrow, and borrow very freely, the more picturesque colloquialisms of America. On informal occasions I sometimes brighten my own speech with phrases which I think I owe to one of the best of living American authors, Mr. George Ade, of Chicago, the author of *Fables in Slang*. The press, the telegraph, the telephone, and the growing habit of travel bind us closer together every year; and the English that we speak, however rich and various it may be, is going to remain one and the same English, our common inheritance.

One question, the most important and difficult of all, remains to be asked. Will this War, in its course and in its effects, tend to prevent or discourage later wars? If the gains that it brings prove to be merely partial and national gains, if it exalts one nation by unjustly depressing another, and conquers cruelty by equal

cruelty, then nothing can be more certain than that the
peace of the world is farther off than ever. When she
was near her death, Edith Cavell, patriot and martyr,
said that patriotism is not enough. Every one who
thinks on international affairs knows this; almost
every one forgets it in time of war. What can be done
to prevent nations from appealing to the wild justice of
revenge?

A League of Nations may do good, but I am surprised
that any one who has imagination and a knowledge of
the facts should entertain high hopes of it as a full
solution. There is a League of Nations to-day which
has given a verdict against the Central Powers, and
that verdict is being enforced by the most terrible War
in all human history. If the verdict had been given
before the War began, it may be said, then Germany
might have accepted it, and refrained. So she might,
but what then? She would have felt herself wronged;
she would have deferred the War, and, in ways that she
knows so well, would have set about making a party for
herself among the nations of the League. Who can be
confident that she would have failed either to divide her
judges, or to accumulate such elements of strength that
she might dare to defy them? A League of Nations
would work well only if its verdicts were loyally accepted
by all the nations composing it. To make majority-rule
possible you must have a community made up of members who are reasonably well informed upon one another's
affairs, and who are bound together by a tie of loyalty
stronger and more enduring than their causes of difference. It would be a happy thing if the nations of the
world made such a community; and the sufferings of

this War have brought them nearer to desiring it.   But
those who believe that such a community can be formed
to-day or to-morrow are too sanguine.   It must not be
forgotten that the very principle of the League, if its
judgements are to take effect, involves a world-war in
cases where a strong minority resists those judgements.
Every war would become a world-war.   Perhaps this
very fact would prevent wars, but it cannot be said that
experience favours such a conclusion.

There is no escape for us by way of the Gospels.   The
Gospel precept to turn the other cheek to the aggressor
was not addressed to a meeting of trustees.   Christianity
has never shirked war, or even much disliked it.   Where
the whole soul is set on things unseen, wounds and death
become of less account.   And if the Christians have not
helped us to avoid war, how should the pacifists be of
use?   Those of them whom I happen to know, or to have
met, have shown themselves, in the relations of civil life,
to be irritable, self-willed, combative creatures, where the
average soldier is calm, unselfish, and placable.   There
is something incongruous and absurd in the pacifist of
British descent.   He has fighting in his blood, and
when his creed, or his nervous sensibility to physical
horrors, denies him the use of fighting, his blood turns
sour.   He can argue, and object, and criticize, but he
cannot lead.   All that he can offer us in effect is eternal
quarrels in place of occasional fights.

No one can do anything to prevent war who does
not recognize its splendour, for it is by its splendour
that it keeps its hold on humanity, and persists.   The
wickedest and most selfish war in the world is not
fought by wicked and selfish soldiers.   The spirit of

man is immense, and for an old memory, a pledged word, a sense of fellowship, offers this frail and complicated tissue of flesh and blood, which a pin or a grain of sand will disorder, to be the victim of all the atrocities that the wit of man can compound out of fire and steel and poison. If that spirit is to be changed, or directed into new courses, it must be by one who understands it, and approaches it reverently, with bared head.

The best hope seems to me to lie in paying chief attention to the improvement of war rather than to its abolition; to the decencies of the craft; to the style rather than the matter. Style is often more important than matter, and this War would not have been so fierce or so prolonged if it had not become largely a war on a point of style, a war, that is to say, to determine the question how war should be waged. If the Germans had behaved humanely and considerately to the civil population of Belgium, if they had kept their solemn promise not to use poison-gas, if they had refrained from murder at sea, if their valour had been accompanied by chivalry, the War might now have been ended, perhaps not in their disfavour, for it would not have been felt, as it now is felt, that they must be defeated at no matter how great a cost, or civilization will perish.

Even as things are, there have been some gains in the manner of conducting war, which, when future generations look back on them, will be seen to be considerable. It is true that modern science has devised new and appalling weapons. The invention of a new weapon in war always arouses protest, but it does not usually, in the long run, make war more inhuman.

There was a great outcry in Europe when the broad-sword was superseded by the rapier, and a tall man of his hands could be spitted like a cat or a rabbit by any dexterous little fellow with a trained wrist.   There was a wave of indignation, which was a hundred years in passing, when musketry first came into use, and a man-at-arms of great prowess could be killed from behind a wall by one who would not have dared to meet him in open combat.   But these changes did not, in effect, make war crueller or more deadly.   They gave more play to intelligence, and abolished the tyranny of the bully, who took the wall of every man he met, and made him-self a public nuisance.   The introduction of poison-gas, which is a small thing compared with the invention of fire-arms, has given the chemist a place in the ranks of fighting-men.   And if science has lent its aid to the destruction of life, it has spent greater zeal and more prolonged effort on the saving of life.   No previous war will compare with this in care for the wounded and maimed.   In all countries, and on all fronts, an army of skilled workers devote themselves to this single end.   I believe that this quickening of the human con-science, for that is what it is, will prove to be the greatest gain of the War, and the greatest advance made in restraint of war.   If the nations come to recognize that their first duty, and their first responsibility, is to those who give so much in their service, that recognition will of itself do more than can be done by any conclave of statesmen to discourage war.   It was the monk Telemachus, according to the old story, who stopped the gladiatorial games at Rome, and was stoned by the people.   If war, in process of time, shall be abolished, or, failing that, shall be governed by the codes of humanity and chivalry, like a decent tournament ; then the one sacrificial figure which will everywhere be honoured for the change will be the figure not of a priest or a politician, but of a hospital nurse.

THE WAR AND THE PRESS

A paper read to the Essay Society, Eton College,
March 14, 1918.

WHEN you asked me to read or speak to you,
I promised to speak about the War. What I have
to say is wholly orthodox, but it is none the worse
for that. Indeed, when I think how entirely the War
possesses our thoughts and how entirely we are agreed
concerning it, I seem to see a new meaning in the
creeds of the religions. These creeds grew up by
general consent, and no one who believed them grudged
repeating them. In the face of an indifferent or hostile
world the faithful found themselves obliged to define
their belief, and to strengthen themselves by an un-
wearying and united profession of faith. It is the
enemy who gives meaning to a religious creed : without our creed we cannot win. So I am willing to
remind you of what you know, rather than to try to
introduce you to novelties.

The strength of the enemy lies in his creed ; not in
the lands that he has ravished from his neighbours.
If his creed does not prevail, his lands will not help
him. Germany has taken lands from Belgium, Serbia,
Roumania, Russia, and the rest, but unless her diges-
tion is as strong as her appetite, she will fail to keep
them. If she is to hold them in peace, the peoples

who inhabit these lands must be either exterminated or converted to the German creed. Lands can be annexed by a successful campaign; they can be permanently conquered only by the operations of peace. The people who survive will be a weakness to the German Empire unless they accept what they are offered, a share in the German creed.

That creed has not many natural attractions for the peoples on whom it is imposed by force. It is an intensely patriotic creed; it insists on racial supremacy, and on unity to be achieved by violence. Pleading and persuasion have little part in it except as instruments of deceit. There is no use in listening to what the Germans say; they do not believe it themselves. What they say is for others; what they do is for themselves. While they are at war, language for them has only two uses—to conceal their thoughts, and to deceive their enemies.

The creed of Western civilization, for which they feel nothing but contempt, and on which they will be broken, is not a simple thing, like theirs. The words by which it is commonly expressed—democracy, parliamentarism, individual liberty, diversity, free development—are puzzling theoretic words, which make no instinctive appeal to the heart. Nevertheless, we stand for growth as against order; and for life as against death. If Germany wins this war, her system will have to be broken or to decay before growth can start again. Must we lose even a hundred years in shaking ourselves free from the paralysis of the German nightmare?

The Germans have shown themselves strong in their

unity, and strong in their willingness to make great
sacrifices to preserve that unity. No one can deny
nobility to the sacrifice made by the simple-minded
German soldier who dies fighting bravely for his
people and his creed. His narrowness is his strength,
and makes unselfishness easier by saving his mind
from question. 'This one thing you shall do', his
country says to him, 'fight and die for your country,
so that your country and your people shall have lord-
ship over other countries and other peoples. You are
nothing; Germany is everything.'

We who live in this island love our country with at
least as deep a passion; but a creed so simple as the
German creed will never do for us. We are patriotic,
but our patriotism is often overlaid and confused by
a wider thought and a wider sympathy than the
Germans have ever known. Much extravagant praise
has lately been given to the German power of thinking,
which produces the elaborate marvels of German
organization. But this thinking is slave-thinking,
not master-thinking; it spends itself wholly on
devising complicated means to achieve a very simple
end. That is what makes the Germans so like the
animals. Their wisdom is all cunning. I have had
German friends, two or three, in the course of my life,
but none of them ever understood a word that I said
if I tried to say what I thought. You could talk to
them about food, and they responded easily. It was
all very restful and pleasant, like talking to an
intelligent dog.

If each of the allied nations were devoted to the
creed of nationalism, the alliance could not endure.

We depend for our strength on what we hold in common. The weakness of this wider creed is that it makes no such immediate and strong appeal to the natural instincts as is made by the mother-country. It demands the habitual exercise of reason and imagination. Further, seeing that we are infinitely less tame and less docile than the Germans, we depend for our strength on informing and convincing our people, and on obtaining agreement among them. Questions which in Germany are discussed only in the gloomy Berlin head-quarters of the General Staff are discussed here in the newspapers. In the press, even under the censorship, we think aloud. It records our differences and debates our policy. You could not suppress these differences and these debates without damaging our cause. There is no freedom worth having which does not, sooner or later, include the freedom to say what you think.

No doubt we could, if necessary, carry on for a time without the press; and I agree with those newspaper writers who have been saying recently that the importance of the press is monstrously exaggerated by some of its critics. The working-man, so far as I know him, does not depend for his patriotism on the leader-writers of the newspapers. He takes even the news with a very large grain of salt. 'So the papers say', he remarks; 'it may be true or it may not.' Yet the press has done good service, and might do better, in putting the meaning of the War before our people and in holding them together. Freedom means that we must love our diversity well enough to be willing to unite to protect it. We must die for our

differences as cheerfully as the Germans die for their
pattern.   Or, if we can sketch a design of our cause,
we must be as passionate in defence of that large
vague design as the Germans are passionate in defence
of their tight uniformity and their drill.   If we were
to fail to keep together, our cause, I believe, would
still prevail, but at a cost that we dare not contem-
plate, by way of anarchy, and the dissolution of
societies, by long tortures, and tears, and martyrdoms.
If we refuse to die in the ranks against the German
tyranny we can keep our faith by dying at the stake.
There are those who think martyrdom the better way;
and certainly that was how Christianity prevailed in
Europe; you can read the story in Caxton's transla-
tion of the *Golden Legend*.   But these saints and
martyrs were making a beginning; we are fighting
to keep what we have won, and it would be a huge
failure on our part if we could keep nothing of it, but
had to begin all over again.

The business of the press, then, at this present
crisis, is to keep the cause for which we are fighting
clearly before us, and this it has done well; also,
because we do not fight best in blinders, to tell us all
that can be known of the facts of the situation, and
this it has done not so well.

The power of the newspapers is that most people
read them, and that many people read nothing else.
Their weakness is that they have to sell or cease to
be, so that by a natural instinct of self-preservation
they fall back on the two sure methods whereby you
can always capture the attention of the public.   Any
man who is trying to say what he thinks, making full

allowance for all doubts and differences, runs the risk of losing his audience. He can regain their attention by flattering them or by frightening them. Flattery and fright, the one following the other from day to day, and often from paragraph to paragraph, is a very large part of the newspaper reader's diet. If he is a sane and busy man, he is not too much impressed by either. He is not mercurial enough for the quick changes of an orator's or journalist's fancy, whereby he is called on, one day, to dig the German warships like rats out of their harbour, and, not many days later, to spend his last shilling on the purchase of the last bullet to shoot at the German invader. He knows that this is such stuff as dreams are made of. He knows also that the orator or journalist, after calling on him for these achievements, goes home to dinner. No great harm is done, just as no great harm is done by bad novels. But an opportunity is lost; the press and the platform might do more than they do to strengthen us and inform us, and help forward our cause.

I name the press and the platform together because they are essentially the same thing. Journalism is a kind of talk. The press, it is fair to say, is ourselves; and every people, it may truly be said, has the press that it deserves. But reading is a thing that we do chiefly for indulgence and pleasure in our idle time; and the press falls in with our mood, and supplies us with what we want in our weaker and lazier moments. No responsible man, with an eager and active mind, spends much of his time on the newspapers. Those who are excited to action by what

they read in the papers are mostly content with the
mild exercise of writing to these same papers to
explain that some one else ought to do something
and to do it at once. Their excitement worries themselves more than it hurts others. When the devil,
with horns and hooves, appeared to Cuvier, the
naturalist, and threatened to devour him, Cuvier, who
was asleep at the time, opened his eyes and looked at
the terrible apparition. 'Hm,' he said, ' cloven-footed;
graminivorous; needn't be afraid of you;' and he
went to sleep again. A man who says that he has
not time to read the morning papers carefully is
commonly a man who counts; he knows what he
has to do, and he goes on doing it. So far as I have
observed, the cadets who are training for command in
the army take very little interest in the exhortations
of the newspapers. They even prefer the miserable
trickle which is all that is left of football news.

One of the chief problems connected with the press
is therefore this—how can it be prevented from producing hysteria in the feeble-minded? In time of
war the censorship no doubt does something to prevent this; and I think it might do more. 'Scare-
lines', as they are called—that is, sensational headings
in large capital letters—might be reduced by law to
modest dimensions. More important, the censorship
might insist that all who write shall sign their
names to their articles. Why should journalists
alone be relieved of responsibility to their country?
Is it possible that the Government is afraid of the
press? There is no need for fear. 'Beware of Aris-
tophanes', says Landor, 'he can cast your name as

a byword to a thousand cities of Asia for a thousand years.' But all that the press can do by its disfavour is to keep your name obscure in a hundred cities of England for a hundred days. Signed articles are robbed of their vague impressiveness, and are known for what they are—the opinions of one man. I would also recommend that a photograph of the author be placed at the head of every article. I have been saved from many bad novels by the helpful pictorial advertisements of modern publishers.

The real work of the Press, as I said, is to help to hold the people together. Nothing else that it can do is of any importance compared with this. We are at one in this War as we have never been at one before within living memory, as we were not at one against Napoleon or against Louis XIV. Our trial is on us; and if we cannot preserve our oneness, we fail. What would be left to us I do not know ; but I am sure that an England which had accepted conditions of peace at Germany's hands would not be the England that any of us know. There might still be a few Englishmen, but they would have to look about for somewhere to live. Serbia would be a good place; it has made no peace-treaty with Germany.

We are profoundly at one; and are divided only by illusions, which the press, in times past, has done much to keep alive. One of these illusions is the illusion of party. I have never been behind the scenes, among the creaking machinery, but 'my impression, as a spectator, is that parties in England are made very much as you pick up sides for a game. I have observed that they are all conservative. The affections are conservative ; every one has a liking for his old habits and his old associates.   There is something comic in a well-nourished rich man who believes that he is a bold reformer and a destructive thinker. For real clotted reactionary sentiment I know nothing to match the table-talk of any aged parliamentary Radical.   When we get a Labour Government, it will be patriotic, prejudiced, opposed to all innovation, superstitiously reverential of the past, sticky and, probably, tyrannical.

The party illusion has been much weakened by the War, and those who still repeat the old catch-words are very near to lunacy.   There is a deeper and more dangerous illusion which has not been killed—the class illusion.   We are all very much alike ; but we live in water-tight compartments called classes, and the inhabitants of each compartment tend to believe that they alone are patriotic.   This illusion, to be just, is not fostered chiefly by the press, which wants to sell its work to all classes ; but it has strong hold of the Government office.   The Government does not know the people, except as an actor knows the audience ; and therefore does not trust the people.   It is pathetic to hear officials talking timidly of the people—will they endure hardships and sacrifices, will they carry through ?   Yet most of the successes we have won in the War have to be credited not so much to the skill of the management as to the amazing high courage of the ordinary soldier and sailor. Even soldiers are often subject to class illusion. I remember listening, in the first month of the War, to a retired colonel, who explained, with some heat,

that the territorials could never be of any use. That
illusion has gone. Then it was Kitchener's army—
well-meaning people, no doubt, but impossible for
a European war. Kitchener's army made good. Now
it is the civil population, who, though they are the
blood relatives of the soldiers, are distrusted, and
believed to be likely to fail under a strain. Yet all
the time, if you want to hear half-hearted, timid,
pusillanimous talk, the place where you are most
likely to hear it is in the public offices. Most of
those who talk in this way would be brave enough in
fight, but they are kept at desks, and worried with
detailed business, and harassed by speculative dangers,
and they lose perspective. Soon or late, we are going
to win this War ; and it is the people who are going
to win it.

If the press (or perhaps the Government, which
controls the press) is not afraid of the people, why
does it tell them so little about our reverses, and the
merits of our enemies? For information concerning
these things we have to depend wholly on conversation with returned soldiers. For instance, the horrible
stories that we hear of the brutal treatment of our
prisoners are numerous, and are true, and make a
heavy bill against Germany, which bill we mean to
present. But are they fair examples of the average
treatment ? We cannot tell ; the accounts published are
almost exclusively confined to the worst happenings.
Most of the officers with whom I have talked who had
been in several German military prisons said that they
had nothing serious to complain of. Prison is not a
good place, and it is not pleasant to have your pea-

soup and your coffee, one after the other, in the same
tin dipper; but they were soldiers, and they agreed
that it would be absurd to make a grievance of things
like that. One private soldier was an even greater
philosopher. 'No', he said, 'I have nothing to complain of. Of course, they do spit at you a good deal.'
That man was unconquerable.

In shipping returns and the like we are given
averages; why are we told nothing at all of the
milder experiences of our soldier prisoners? It would
not make us less resolved to do all that we can to
better the lot of those who are suffering insult and
torture, and to exact full retribution from the enemy.
And it would bring some hope to those whose husbands
or children or friends are in German military prisons,
and who are racked every day by tales of what, in
fact, are exceptional atrocities.

Or take the question of the conduct of German
officers. We know that the Prussian military Government, in its approved handbooks, teaches its officers
the use of brutality and terror as military weapons.
The German philosophy of war, of which this is a
part, is not really a philosophy of war; it is a philosophy of victory. For a long time now the Germans
have been accustomed to victory, and have studied
the arts of breaking the spirit and torturing the mind
of the peoples whom they invade. Their philosophy
of war will have to be rewritten when the time comes
for them to accommodate their doctrine to their own
defeat. In the meantime they teach frightfulness to
their officers, and most of their officers prove ready
pupils. There must be some, one would think, here

and there, if only a sprinkling, who fall short of the
Prussian doctrine, and are betrayed by human feeling
into what we should recognize as decent and honourable conduct.   And so there are; only we do not hear
of them through the press.   I should like to tell two
stories which come to me from personal sources.   The
first may be called the story of the Christmas truce
and the German captain.   In the lull which fell on
the fighting at the time of the first Christmas of the
War, a British officer was disquieted to notice that his
men were fraternizing with the Germans, who were
standing about with them in No-man's land, laughing
and talking.   He went out to them at once, to bring
them back to their own trenches.   When he came up
to his men, he met a German captain who had arrived
on the same errand.   The two officers, British and
German, fell into talk, and while they were standing
together, in not unfriendly fashion, one of the men
took a snapshot photograph of them, copies of which
were afterwards circulated in the trenches.   Then the
men were recalled to their duty, on the one side and
the other, and, after an interval of some days, the war
began again.   A little time after this the British officer
was in charge of a patrol, and, having lost his way,
found himself in the German trenches, where he and
his men were surrounded and captured.   As they
were being marched off along the trenches, they met
the German captain, who ordered the men to be
taken to the rear, and then, addressing the officer
without any sign of recognition, said in a loud voice,
'You, follow me!'   He led him by complicated ways
along a whole series of trenches and up a sap,

at the end of which he stopped, saluted, and, pointing with his hand, said ' Your trenches are there. Good day.'

My second story, the story of the British lieutenant in No-man's land, is briefer. I was with a friend of mine, a young officer back from the front, wounded, and the conduct of German officers was being discussed. He said, 'You can't expect me to be very hard on German officers, for one of them saved my life'. He then told how he and a companion crept out into No-man's land to bring in some of our wounded who were lying there. When they had reached the wounded, and were preparing to bring them in, they were discovered by the Germans opposite, who at once whipped up a machine-gun and turned it on them. Their lives were not worth half a minute's purchase, when suddenly a German officer leapt up on to the parapet, and, angrily waving back the machine-gunners, called out, in English, ' That 's all right. You may take them in.'

These are no doubt exceptional cases ; the rule is very different. But a good many of such cases are known to soldiers, and I have seen none of them in the press. Soldiers are silent by law, and journalists either do not hear these things, or, believing that hate is a valuable asset, suppress all mention of them. If England could ever be disgraced by a mishap, she would be disgraced by having given birth to those Englishmen, few and wretched, who, when an enemy behaves generously, conceal or deny the fact. And consider the effect of this silence on the Germans. There are some German officers, as I said, who are

better than the German military handbooks, and
better than their monstrous chiefs. Which of them
will pay the smallest attention to what our papers say
when he finds that they collect only atrocities, and
are blind to humanity if they see it in an enemy?
He will regard our press accounts of the German
army as the work of malicious cripples ; and our perfectly true narrative of the unspeakable brutality and
filthiness of the German army's doings will lose credit
with him.

If I had my way, I would staff the newspaper
offices, as far as possible, with wounded soldiers, and
I would give some of the present staff a holiday as
stretcher-bearers. Then we should hear more of the
truth.

Is it feared that we should have no heart for the
War if once we are convinced that among the
Germans there are some human beings ? Is it believed
that our people can be heroic on one condition only,
that they shall be asked to fight no one but orang-
outangs ? Our airmen fight as well as any one, in this
world or above it, has ever fought ; and we owe them
a great debt of thanks for maintaining, and, by their
example, actually teaching the Germans to maintain,
a high standard of decency.

This War has shown, what we might have gathered
from our history, that we fight best up hill. From
our history also we may learn that it does not relax
our sinews to be told that our enemy has some good
qualities. We should like him better as an enemy if
he had more. We know what we have believed ; and
we are not going to fail in resolve or perseverance

because we find that our task is difficult, and that we have not a monopoly of all the virtues.

Most of us will not live to see it, for our recovery from this disease will be long and troublesome, but the War will do great things for us. It will make a reality of the British Commonwealth, which until now has been only an aspiration and a dream. It will lay the sure foundation of a League of Nations in the affection and understanding which it has promoted among all English-speaking peoples, and in the relations of mutual respect and mutual service which it has established between the English-speaking peoples and the Latin races. Our united Rolls of Honour make the most magnificent list of benefactors that the world has ever seen. In the end, the War may perhaps even save the soul of the main criminal, awaken him from his bloody dream, and lead him back by degrees to the possibility of innocence and goodwill.

SHAKESPEARE AND ENGLAND

Annual Shakespeare Lecture of the British Academy, delivered July 4, 1918

THERE is nothing new and important to be said of Shakespeare. In recent years antiquaries have made some additions to our knowledge of the facts of his life. These additions are all tantalizing and comparatively insignificant. The history of the publication of his works has also become clearer and more intelligible, especially by the labours of Mr. Pollard; but the whole question of quartos and folios remains thorny and difficult, so that no one can reach any definite conclusion in this matter without a liberal use of conjecture.

I propose to return to the old catholic doctrine which has been illuminated by so many disciples of Shakespeare, and to speak of him as our great national poet. He embodies and exemplifies all the virtues, and most of the faults, of England. Any one who reads and understands him understands England. This method of studying Shakespeare by reading him has perhaps gone somewhat out of vogue in favour of more roundabout ways of approach, but it is the best method for all that. Shakespeare tells us more about himself and his mind than we could learn even from those who knew him in his habit as he lived, if they were all alive and all talking. To learn what he tells we have only to listen.

I think there is no national poet, of any great nation whatsoever, who is so completely representative of his own people as Shakespeare is representative of the English.   There is certainly no other English poet who comes near to Shakespeare in embodying our character and our foibles.   No one, in this connexion, would venture even to mention Spenser or Milton.   Chaucer is English, but he lived at a time when England was not yet completely English, so that he is only half-conscious of his nation.   Wordsworth is English, but he was a recluse.   Browning is English, but he lived apart or abroad, and was a tourist of genius.   The most English of all our great men of letters, next to Shakespeare, is certainly Dr. Johnson, but he was no great poet.   Shakespeare, it may be suspected, is too poetic to be a perfect Englishman; but his works refute that suspicion.   He is the Englishman endowed, by a fortunate chance, with matchless powers of expression.   He is not silent or dull; but he understands silent men, and he enters into the minds of dull men. Moreover, the Englishman seems duller than he is.   It is a point of pride with him not to be witty and not to give voice to his feelings.   The shepherd Corin, who was never in court, has the true philosophy.   ' He that hath learned no wit by nature nor art may complain of good breeding or comes of a very dull kindred.'

Shakespeare knew nothing of the British Empire. He was an islander, and his patriotism was centred on

> This precious stone set in the silver sea,
> Which serves it in the office of a wall,
> Or as a moat defensive to a house,
> Against the envy of less happier lands.

When he speaks of Britons and British he always means the Celtic peoples of the island. Once only he makes a slip. There is a passage in *King Lear* (IV. vi. 249) where the followers of the King, who in the text of the quarto versions are correctly called 'the British party', appear in the folio version as 'the English party'. Perhaps the quartos contain Shakespeare's own correction of his own inadvertence; but those of us, and we are many, who have been blamed by northern patriots for the misuse of the word English may claim Shakespeare as a brother in misfortune.

Our critics, at home and abroad, accuse us of arrogance. I doubt if we can prove them wrong; but they do not always understand the nature of English arrogance. It does not commonly take the form of self-assertion. Shakespeare's casual allusions to our national characteristics are almost all of a kind; they are humorous and depreciatory. Here are some of them. Every holiday fool in England, we learn from Trinculo in *The Tempest*, would give a piece of silver to see a strange fish, though no one will give a doit to relieve a lame beggar. The English are quarrelsome, Master Slender testifies, at the game of bear-baiting. They are great drinkers, says Iago, 'most potent in potting; your Dane, your German, and your swag-bellied Hollander are nothing to your English'. They are epicures, says Macbeth. They will eat like wolves and fight like devils, says the Constable of France. An English nobleman, according to the Lady of Belmont, can speak no language but his own. An English tailor, according to the porter of Macbeth's castle, will steal cloth where there is hardly any cloth to be stolen, out of a French hose. The devil, says the clown in *All's Well*, has an English name; he is called the Black Prince.

Nothing has been changed in this vein of humorous banter since Shakespeare died. One of the best pieces of Shakespeare criticism ever written is contained in four words of the present Poet Laureate's Ode for the Tercentenary of Shakespeare, 'London's laughter is thine'. The wit of our trenches in this war, especially perhaps among the Cockney and South country regiments, is pure Shakespeare. Falstaff would find himself at home there, and would recognize a brother in Old Bill.

The best known of Shakespeare's allusions to England are no doubt those splendid outbursts of patriotism which occur in *King John*, and *Richard II*, and *Henry V*. And of these the dying speech of John of Gaunt, in *Richard II*, is the deepest in feeling. It is a lament upon the decay of England, 'this dear, dear land'. Since we began to be a nation we have always lamented our decay. I am afraid that the Germans, whose self-esteem takes another form, were deceived by this. To the right English temper all bragging is a thing of evil omen. That temper is well expressed, where perhaps you would least expect to find it, in the speech of King Henry V to the French herald:

> To say the sooth,—
> Though 'tis no wisdom to confess so much
> Unto an enemy of craft and vantage,—
> My people are with sickness much enfeebled,
> My numbers lessened, and those few I have

Almost no better than so many French;
Who, when they were in health, I tell thee, herald,
I thought upon one pair of English legs
Did march three Frenchmen.   Yet, forgive me, God,
That I do brag thus! This your air of France
Hath blown that vice in me; I must repent.
Go therefore, tell thy master here I am:
My ransom is this frail and worthless trunk;
My army but a weak and sickly guard;
Yet, God before, tell him we will come on,
Though France himself and such another neighbour
Stand in our way.   There's for thy labour, Montjoy.
Go bid thy master well advise himself:
If we may pass, we will; if we be hindered,
We shall your tawny ground with your red blood
Discolour; and so, Montjoy, fare you well.
The sum of all our answer is but this:
We would not seek a battle as we are;
Nor, as we are, we say we will not shun it;
So tell your master.

That speech might have been written for the war
which we are waging to-day against a less honourable
enemy.   But, indeed, Shakespeare is full of prophecy.
Here is his description of the volunteers who flocked
to the colours in the early days of the war:

Rash inconsiderate fiery voluntaries,
With ladies' faces and fierce dragons' spleens,
Have sold their fortunes at their native homes,
Bearing their birthrights proudly on their backs,
To make a hazard of new fortunes here.
In brief, a braver choice of dauntless spirits
Than now the English bottoms have waft o'er
Did never float upon the swelling tide.

And here is his sermon on national unity, preached
by the Bishop of Carlisle:

O, if you rear this house against this house,
It will the woefullest division prove
That ever fell upon this cursed earth.
Prevent it, resist it, let it not be so,
Lest child, child's children, cry against you 'Woe!'

The patriotism of the women is described by the Bastard in *King John*:

Your own ladies and pale-visag'd maids
Like Amazons come tripping after drums:
Their thimbles into armed gauntlets change,
Their needles to lances, and their gentle hearts
To fierce and bloody inclination.

Lastly, Queen Isabella's blessing, spoken over King Henry V and his French bride, predicts an enduring friendship between England and France:

As man and wife, being two, are one in love,
So be there 'twixt your kingdoms such a spousal,
That never may ill office, or fell jealousy,
Which troubles oft the bed of blessed marriage,
Thrust in between the paction of these kingdoms,
To make divorce of their incorporate league;
That English may as French, French Englishmen,
Receive each other! God speak this Amen!

One of the delights of a literature as rich and as old as ours is that at every step we take backwards we find ourselves again. We are delivered from that foolish vein of thought, so dear to ignorant conceit, which degrades the past in order to exalt the present and the future. It is easy to feel ourselves superior to men who no longer breathe and walk, and whom we do not trouble to understand. Here is the real benefit of scholarship; it reduces men to kinship with their race. Science, pressing forward, and beating against the bars which guard the secrets of the future, has no such sympathy in its gift.

Anyhow, in Shakespeare's time, England was already old England; which if she could ever cease to be, she might be Jerusalem, or Paradise, but would not be England at all. What Shakespeare and his fellows of the sixteenth century gave her was a new self-consciousness and a new self-confidence. They foraged in the past; they recognized themselves in their ancestors; they found feudal England, which had existed for many hundreds of years, a dumb thing; and when she did not know her own meaning, they endowed her purposes with words. They gave her a new delight in herself, a new sense of power and exhilaration, which has remained with her to this day, surviving all the airy philosophic theories of humanity which thought to supersede the old solid national temper. The English national temper is better fitted for traffic with the world than any mere doctrine can ever be, for it is marked by an immense tolerance. And this, too, Shakespeare has expressed. Falstaff is perhaps the most tolerant man who was ever made in God's image. But it is rather late in the day to introduce Falstaff to an English audience. Perhaps you will let me modernize a brief scene from Shakespeare, altering nothing essential, to illustrate how completely his spirit is the spirit of our troops in Flanders and France.

A small British expeditionary force, bound on an international mission, finds itself stranded in an unknown country. The force is composed of men very various in rank and profession. Two of them, whom

we may call a non-commissioned officer and a private,
go exploring by themselves, and take one of the natives
of the place prisoner. This native is an ugly low-born
creature, of great physical strength and violent criminal
tendencies, a liar, and ready at any time for theft, rape,
and murder. He is a child of Nature, a lover of music,
slavish in his devotion to power and rank, and very
easily imposed upon by authority. His captors do not
fear him, and, which is more, they do not dislike him.
They found him lying out in a kind of no-man's land,
drenched to the skin, so they determine to keep him
as a souvenir, and to take him home with them. They
nickname him, in friendly fashion, the monster, and
the mooncalf, as who should say Fritz, or the Boche.
But their first care is to give him a drink, and to
make him swear allegiance upon the bottle. ' Where
the devil should he learn our language ? ' says the non-
commissioned officer, when the monster speaks. ' I will
give him some relief, if it be but for that.' The prisoner
then offers to kiss the foot of his captor. ' I shall laugh
myself to death ', says the private, ' at this puppy-
headed monster. A most scurvy monster ! I could
find in my heart to beat him, but that the poor
monster's in drink.' When the private continues to
rail at the monster, his officer calls him to order.
' Trinculo, keep a good tongue in your head : if you
prove a. mutineer, the next tree—— The poor
monster's my subject, and he shall not suffer
indignity.'

In this scene from *The Tempest* everything is
English except the names. The incident has been
repeated many times in the last four years. ' This

is Bill,' one private said, introducing a German soldier
to his company. 'He's my prisoner. I wounded him,
and I took him, and where I go he goes. Come on,
Bill, old man.' The Germans have known many failures
since they began the War, but one failure is more tragic
than all the rest. They love to be impressive, to produce a panic of apprehension and a thrill of reverence
in their enemy; and they have completely failed to
impress the ordinary British private. He remains
incurably humorous, and so little moved to passion
that his daily offices of kindness are hardly inter-
rupted.

Shakespeare's tolerance, which is no greater than
the tolerance of the common English soldier, may be
well seen in his treatment of his villains. Is a liar,
or a thief, merely a bad man? Shakespeare does not
much encourage you to think so. Is a murderer a bad
man? He would be an undiscerning critic who should
accept that phrase as a true and adequate description
of Macbeth. Shakespeare does not dislike liars, thieves,
and murderers as such, and he does not pretend to
dislike them. He has his own dislikes. I once asked
a friend of mine, long since dead, who refused to
condemn almost anything, whether there were any
vices that he could not find it in his heart to tolerate.
He replied at once that there were two—cruelty, and
bilking; which, if the word is not academic, I may
paraphrase as cheating the helpless, swindling a child
out of its pennies, or leaving a house by the back door
in order to avoid paying your cabman his lawful fare.
These exclusions from mercy Shakespeare would accept;
and I think he would add a third. His worst villains

are all theorists, who cheat and murder by the book. of arithmetic. They are men of principle, and are ready to expound their principle and to defend it in argument. They follow it, without remorse or mitigation, wherever it leads them. It is Iago's logic that makes him so terrible; his mind is as cold as a snake and as hard as a surgeon's knife. The Italian Renaissance did produce some such men; the modern German imitation is a grosser and feebler thing, brutality trying to emulate the glitter and flourish of refined cruelty.

With his wonderful quickness of intuition and his unsurpassed subtlety of expression Shakespeare drew the characters of the Englishmen that he saw around him. Why is it that he has given us no full-length portrait, carefully drawn, of a hypocrite? It can hardly have been for lack of models. Outside England, not only among our enemies, but among our friends and allies, it is agreed that hypocrisy is our national vice, our ruling passion. There must be some meaning in so widely held an opinion; and, on our side, there are damaging admissions by many witnesses. The portrait gallery of Charles Dickens is crowded with hypocrites. Some of them are greasy and servile, like Mr. Pumblechook or Uriah Heep; others rise to poetic heights of daring, like Mr. Chadband or Mr. Squeers. But Shakespeare's hypocrites enjoy themselves too much; they are artists to the fingertips. It may be said, no doubt, that Shakespeare lived before organized religious dissent had developed a new type of character among the weaker brethren. But the Low Church Protestant, whom Shakespeare certainly knew, is not very different from the evan-

I

gelical dissenter of later days; and he did not interest
Shakespeare.

My own impression is that Shakespeare had a free
and happy childhood, and grew up without much
check from his elders. It is the child who sees
hypocrites. These preposterous grown-up people,
who, if they are well-mannered, do not seem to
enjoy their food, who are fussy about meaningless
employments, and never give way to natural impulses,
must surely assume this veil of decorum with intent
to deceive. Charles Dickens was hard driven in his
childhood, and the impressions that were then burnt
into him governed all his seeing. The creative spirit
in him transformed his sufferings into delight; but
he never outgrew them; and, when he died, the eyes
of a child were closed upon a scene touched, it is true,
here and there with rapturous pleasure, rich in oddity,
and trembling with pathos, but, in the main, as bleak
and unsatisfying as the wards of a workhouse. The
intense emotions of his childhood made the usual
fervours of adolescence a faint thing in the comparison, and if you want to know how lovers think
and feel you do not go to Dickens to tell you. You
go to Shakespeare, who put his childhood behind him,
so that he almost forgot it, and ran forward to seize
life with both hands. He sometimes looked back on
children, and saw them through the eyes of their
elders. Dickens saw men and women as they appear
to children.

This comparison suggests a certain lack of sympathy
or lack of understanding in those who are quick to
see hypocrisy in others. In Dickens lack of sym-

pathy was a fair revenge; moreover, his hypocrites
amused him so much that he did not wish to understand them. What a loss it would have been to the
world if he had explained them away! But it is
difficult, I think, to see a hypocrite in a man whose
intimacy you have cultivated, whose mind you have
entered into, as Shakespeare entered into the mind
of his creatures. Hypocrisy, in its ordinary forms,
is a superficial thing—a skin disease, not a cancer.
It is not easy, at best, to bring the outward and
inward relations of the soul into perfect harmony;
a hypocrite is one who too readily consents to their
separation. The English, for I am ready now to
return to my point, are a people of a divided mind,
slow to drive anything through on principle, very
ready to find reason in compromise. They are
passionate, and they are idealists, but they are also
a practical people, and they dare not give the rein
to a passion or an idea. They know that in this
world an unmitigated principle simply will not work;
that a clean cut will never take you through the
maze. So they restrain themselves, and listen, and
seem patient. They are not so patient as they seem;
they must be hypocrites! A cruder, simpler people
like the Germans feel indignation, not unmixed
perhaps with envy, when they hear the quiet voice
and see the white lips of the thoroughbred Englishman who is angry. It is not manly or honest, they
think, to be angry without getting red in the face.
They certainly feel pride in their own honesty when
they give explosive vent to heir emotions. They
have not learned the elements of self-distrust. The

Englishman is seldom quite content to be himself;
often his thoughts are troubled by something better.
He suffers from the divided mind; and earns the
reputation of a hypocrite. But the simpler nature
that indulges itself and believes in itself has an even
heavier penalty to pay. If, in the name of honesty,
you cease to distinguish between what you are and
what you would wish to be, between how you act
and how you would like to act, you are in some
danger of reeling back into the beast. It is true that
man is an animal; and before long you feel a glow
of conscious virtue in proclaiming and illustrating
that truth. You scorn the hypocrisy of pretending
to be better than you are, and that very scorn fixes
you in what you are. 'He that is unjust, let him
be unjust still; and he which is filthy, let him be
filthy still.' That is the epitaph on German honesty.

I have drifted away from Shakespeare, who knew
nothing of the sea of troubles that England would
one day take arms against, and who could not know
that on that day she would outgo his most splendid
praise and more than vindicate his reverence and his
affection. But Shakespeare is still so live a mind
that it is vain to try to expound him by selected
texts, or to pin him to a mosaic of quotations from
his book. Often, if you seek to know what he
thought on questions which must have exercised
his imagination, you can gather it only from a hint,
dropped by accident, and quite irrelevant. What
were his views on literature, and on the literary
controversies which have been agitated from his day
to our own? He tells us very little. He must have

heard discussions and arguments on metre, on classical precedent, on the ancient and modern drama; but he makes no mention of these questions. He does not seem to have attached any prophetic importance to poetry. The poets who exalt their craft are of a more slender build. Is it conceivable that he would have given his support to a literary academy,—a project which began to find advocates during his lifetime? I think not. It is true that he is full of good sense, and that an academy exists to promulgate good sense. Moreover his own free experiments brought him nearer and nearer into conformity with classical models. *Othello* and *Macbeth* are better constructed plays than *Hamlet*. The only one of his plays which, whether by chance or by design, observes the so-called unities, of action and time and place, is one of his latest plays—*The Tempest*. But he was an Englishman, and would have been jealous of his freedom and independence. When the grave-digger remarks that it is no great matter if Hamlet do not recover his wits in England, because there the men are as mad as he, the satire has a sympathetic ring in it. Shakespeare did not wish to see the mad English altered. Nor are they likely to alter; our fears and our hopes are vain. We entered on the greatest of our wars with an army no bigger, so we are told, than the Bulgarian army. Since that time we have regimented and organized our people, not without success; and our soothsayers are now directing our attention to the danger that after the war we shall be kept in uniform and shall become tame creatures, losing our independence and our spirit of enterprise.

There is nothing that soothsayers will not predict when they are gravelled for lack of matter, but this is the stupidest of all their efforts. The national character is not so flimsy a thing; it has gone through good and evil fortune for hundreds of years without turning a hair. You can make a soldier, and a good soldier, of a humorist; but you cannot militarize him. He remains a free thinker.

New institutions do not flourish in England. The town is a comparatively modern innovation; it has never, so to say, caught on. Most schemes of town-planning are schemes for pretending that you live in the country. This is one of the most persistent of our many hypocrisies. Wherever working people inhabit a street of continuous red-brick cottages, the names that they give to their homes are one long catalogue of romantic lies. The houses have no gardens, and the only prospect that they command is the view of over the way. But read their names— The Dingle, The Elms, Pine Grove, Windermere, The Nook, The Nest. Even social pretence, which is said to be one of our weaknesses, and which may be read in such names as Belvoir or Apsley House, is less in evidence than the Englishman's passion for the country. He cannot bear to think that he lives in a town. He does not much respect the institutions of a town. A policeman, before he has been long in the force, has to face the fact that he is generally regarded as a comic character. The police are Englishmen and good fellows, and they accept a situation which would rouse any continental gendarme to heroic indignation. Mayors, Aldermen, and

Justices of the Peace are comic, and take it not quite
so well. Beadles were so wholly dedicated to the
purposes of comedy that I suppose they found their
position unendurable and went to earth; at any rate
it is very difficult to catch one in his official costume.

All this is reflected in Shakespeare. He knew the
country, and he knew the town; and he has not left
it in doubt which was the cherished home of his
imagination. He preferred the fields to the streets,
but the Arcadia of his choice is not agricultural or
even pastoral; it is rather a desert island, or the
uninhabited stretches of wild and woodland country.
Indeed, he has both described it and named it.
'Where will the old Duke live?' says Oliver in
As You Like It. 'They say he is already in the
forest of Arden,' says Charles the wrestler, 'and
a many merry men with him; and there they live
like the old Robin Hood of England. They say
many young gentlemen flock to him every day, and
fleet the time carelessly, as they did in the golden
world.' That is Shakespeare's Arcadia; and who
that has read *As You Like It* will deny that it
breathes the air of Paradise?

It is quite plain that the freedom that Shakespeare
valued was in fact freedom, not any of those ingenious mechanisms to which that name has been
applied by political theorists. He thought long and
profoundly on the problems of society; and anarchy
has no place among his political ideals. It is by all
means to be avoided—at a cost. But what harm would
anarchy do if it meant no more than freedom for
all the impulses of the enlightened imagination and

the tender heart? The ideals of his heart were not
political; and when he indulges himself, as he did
in his latest plays, you must look for him in the
wilds; whether on the road near the shepherd's
cottage, or in the cave among the mountains of
Wales, or on the seashore in the Bermudas. The
laws that are imposed upon the intricate relations of
men in society were a weariness to him; and in this
he is thoroughly English. The Englishman has always
been an objector, and he has a right to object, though
it may very well be held that he is too fond of larding
his objection with the plea of conscience. But even
this has a meaning in our annals; as a mere question
of right we are very slow to prefer the claim of the
organized opinions of society to the claim of the
individual conscience. We know that there is no
good in a man who is doing what he does not will
to do. We are not like our poets or our men of
action to be void of inspiration. A gift is nothing
if there is no benevolence in the giver:

For to the noble mind
Rich gifts wax poor when givers prove unkind.

We ask for the impulse as well as the deed. Even
when he is speaking of social obligations Shakespeare
makes his strongest appeal not to force or command,
but to the natural piety of the heart:

If ever you have looked on better days,
If ever been where bells have knolled to church,
If ever sat at any good man's feast,
If ever from your eyelids wiped a tear,
And know what 'tis to pity and be pitied,
Let gentleness my strong enforcement be:
In the which hope I blush, and hide my sword.

So speaks Orlando when the Duke has met his threats with fair words; and he adds an apology:

> Pardon me, I pray you;
> I thought that all things had been savage here,
> And therefore put I on the countenance
> Of stern commandment.

The ultimate law between man and man, according to Shakespeare, is the law of pity. I suppose that most of us have had our ears so dulled by early familiarity with Portia's famous speech, which we probably knew by heart long before we were fit to understand it, that the heavenly quality of it, equal to almost anything in the New Testament, is obscured and lost. There is no remedy but to read it again; to remember that it was conceived in passion; and to notice how the meaning is raised and perfected as line follows line:

> *Portia.*   Then must the Jew be merciful.
> *Shylock.* On what compulsion must I? Tell me
>   that.
> *Portia.* The quality of mercy is not strained.
> It droppeth as the gentle rain from heaven
> Upon the place beneath; it is twice bless'd;
> It blesseth him that gives and him that takes:
> 'Tis mightiest in the mightiest; it becomes
> The throned monarch better than his crown.
> His sceptre shows the force of temporal power,
> The attribute to awe and majesty,
> Wherein doth sit the dread and fear of kings;
> But mercy is above this sceptred sway,
> It is enthroned in the hearts of kings,
> It is an attribute to God himself,
> And earthly power doth then show likest God's

When mercy seasons justice. Therefore, Jew,
Though justice be thy plea, consider this,
That in the course of justice none of us
Should see salvation: we do pray for mercy,
And that same prayer doth teach us all to render
The deeds of mercy.

That speech rises above the strife of nations; it
belongs to humanity. But an Englishman wrote it;
and the author, we may be sure, if he ever met with
the doctrine that a man who is called on to help his
own people is in duty bound to set aside the claims
of humanity, and to stop his ears to the call of mercy,
knew that the doctrine is an invention of the devil,
stupid and angry, as the devil commonly is. There
are hundreds of thousands of Englishmen who, though
they could not have written the speech, yet know all
that it teaches, and act on the knowledge. It is part
of the creed of the Navy. We can speak more confidently than we could have spoken three or four
years ago. We know that not the extremest pressure
of circumstance could ever bring the people of England
to forget all the natural pieties, to permit official
duties to annul private charities, and to join in the
frenzied dance of hate and lust which leads to the
mouth of the pit.

Yet Germany, where all this seems to have happened,
was not very long ago a country where it was easy
to find humanity, and simplicity, and kindness. It
was a country of quiet industry and content, the
home of fairy stories, which Shakespeare himself
would have loved. The Germans of our day have
made a religion of war and terror, and have used

commerce as a means for the treacherous destruction
of the independence and freedom of others. They
were not always like that.   In the fifteenth century
they spread the art of printing through Europe,
for the service of man, by the method of peaceful
penetration. My friend Mr. John Sampson recently
expressed to me a hope that our air-forces would
not bomb Mainz, 'for Mainz', he said, 'is a sacred
place to the bibliographer'. According to a statement published in Cologne in 1499, 'the highly
valuable art of printing was invented first of all in
Germany at Mainz on the Rhine. And it is a great
honour to the German nation that such ingenious
men are to be found among them. . . . And in the
year of our Lord 1450 it was a golden year, and they
began to print, and the first book they printed was the
Bible in Latin: it was printed in a large character,
resembling the types with which the present mass-
books are printed.' Gutenberg, the printer of this
Bible, never mentions his own name, and the only
personal note we have of his, in the colophon of the
Catholicon, printed in 1460, is a hymn in praise of
his city: 'With the aid of the Most High, who
unlooses the tongues of infants and oft-times reveals
to babes that which is hidden from learned men, this
admirable book, the *Catholicon*, was finished in the
year of the incarnation of our Saviour MCCCCLX,
in the foster town of Mainz, a town of the famous
German nation, which God in his clemency, by
granting to it this high illumination of the mind,
has preferred before the other nations of the world.'
  There is something not quite unlike modern Germany

in that; and yet these older activities of the Germans make a strange contrast with their work to-day. It was in the city of Cologne that Caxton first made acquaintance with his craft. Everywhere the Germans spread printing like a new religion, adapting it to existing conditions. In Bavaria they used the skill of the wood-engravers, and at Augsburg, Ulm, and Nuremberg produced the first illustrated printed books. It was two Germans of the old school, Conrad Sweynheym and Arnold Pannartz, who carried the art to Italy, casting the first type in Roman characters, and printing editions of the classics, first in the Benedictine monastery of St. Scholastica at Subiaco, and later at Rome. They also cast the first Greek type. It was three Germans, Gering, Kranz, and Freyburger, who first printed at Paris, in 1470. It was a German who set up the first printing-press in Spain, in 1474. The Germans were once the cherishers, as now they are the destroyers, of the inheritance of civilization. I do not pretend to explain the change. Perhaps it is a tragedy of education. That is a dangerous moment in the life of a child when he begins to be uneasily aware that he is valued for his simplicity and innocence. Then he resolves to break with the past, to put away childish things, to forgo affection, and to earn respect by imitating the activities of his elders. The strange power of words and the virtues of abstract thought begin to fascinate him. He loses touch with the things of sense, and ceases to speak as a child. If his first attempts at argument and dogma win him praise and esteem, if he proves himself a better fighter than an older boy next door, who has often bullied him, and if at the same time he comes into money, he is on the road to ruin. His very simplicity is a snare to him. 'What a fool I was', he thinks, 'to let myself be put upon; I now see that I am a great philosopher and a splendid soldier, born to subdue others rather than to agree with them, and entitled to a chief share in all the luxuries of the world. It is for me to say what is good and true, and if any of these people contradict me I shall knock them down.' He suits his behaviour to his new conception of himself, and is soon hated by all the neighbours. Then he turns bitter. These people, he thinks, are all in a plot against him. They must be blind to goodness and beauty, or why do they dislike him? His rage reaches the point of madness; he stabs and poisons the villagers, and burns down their houses. We are still waiting to see what will become of him.

This outbreak has been long preparing. Seventy years before the War the German poet Freiligrath wrote a poem to prove that Germany is Hamlet, urged by the spirit of her fathers to claim her inheritance, vacillating and lost in thought, but destined, before the Fifth Act ends, to strew the stage with the corpses of her enemies. Only a German could have hit on the idea that Germany is Hamlet. The English, for whom the play was written, know that Hamlet is Hamlet, and that Shakespeare was thinking of a young man, not of the pomposities of national ambition. But if these clumsy allegories must be imposed upon great poets, Germany need not go abroad to seek the likeness of her destiny. Germany is Faust; she desired science and power and pleasure, and to get them on a short lease she paid the price of her soul.

For the present, at any rate, the best thing the
Germans can do with Shakespeare is to leave him
alone. They have divorced themselves from their own
great poets, to follow vulgar half-witted political
prophets. As for Shakespeare, they have studied him
assiduously, with the complete apparatus of criticism,
for a hundred years, and they do not understand the
plainest words of all his teaching.

In England he has always been understood; and it
is only fair, to him and to ourselves, to add that he has
never been regarded first and foremost as a national
poet. His humanity is too calm and broad to suffer
the prejudices and exclusions of international enmities.
The sovereignty that he holds has been allowed to him
by men of all parties. The schools of literature have,
from the very first, united in his praise. Ben Jonson,
who knew him and loved him, was a classical scholar,
and disapproved of some of his romantic escapades,
yet no one will ever outgo Ben Jonson's praise of
Shakespeare.

Triumph, my Britain, thou hast one to show,
To whom all Scenes of Europe homage owe.
He was not of an age, but for all time!

The sects of religion forget their disputes and recognize
the spirit of religion in this profane author. He cannot
be identified with any institution. According to the
old saying, he gave up the Church and took to religion.
He gave up the State, and took to humanity. The
formularies and breviaries to which political and
religious philosophers profess their allegiance were
nothing to him. These formularies are a convenient
shorthand, to save the trouble of thinking. But

Shakespeare always thought. Every question that
he treats is brought out of the realm of abstraction,
and exhibited in its relation to daily life and the
minds and hearts of men. He could never have been
satisfied with such a smug phrase as 'the greatest
happiness of the greatest number'. His mind would
have been eager for details. In what do the greatest
number find their happiness? How far is the happiness of one consistent with the happiness of another?
What difficulties and miscarriages attend the business
of transmuting the recognized materials for happiness
into living human joy? Even these questions he would
not have been content to handle in high philosophic
fashion; he would have insisted on instances, and
would have subscribed to no code that is not carefully
built out of case-law. He knew that sanity is in the
life of the senses; and that if there are some philosophers who are not mad it is because they live a
double life, and have consolations and resources of
which their books tell you nothing. It is the part of
their life which they do not think it worth their while
to mention that would have interested Shakespeare.
He loves to reduce things to their elements. 'Is man
no more than this?' says the old king on the heath,
as he gazes on the naked madman. 'Consider him
well. Thou owest the worm no silk, the beast no
hide, the sheep no wool, the cat no perfume. Ha!
here's three of us are sophisticated! Thou art the
thing itself: unaccommodated man is no more but
such a poor, bare, forked animal as thou art. Off, off,
you lendings!' That is how Shakespeare lays the
mind of man bare, and strips him of his pretences, to

try if he be indeed noble. And he finds that man, naked and weak, hunted by misfortune, liable to all the sins and all the evils that follow frailty, still has faith left to him, and charity. King Lear is still every inch a king.

That is not a little discovery, for when his mind came to grips with human life Shakespeare did not deal in rhetoric; so that the good he finds is real good—' 'tis in grain; 'twill endure wind and weather'. Nothing is easier than to make a party of humanity, and to exalt mankind by ignorantly vilifying the rest of the animal creation, which is full of strange virtues and abilities. Shakespeare refused that way; he saw man weak and wretched, not able to maintain himself except as a pensioner on the bounty of the world, curiously ignorant of his nature and his destiny, yet endowed with certain gifts in which he can find sustenance and rest, brave by instinct, so that courage is not so much his virtue as cowardice is his lamentable and exceptional fault, ready to forget his pains or to turn them into pleasures by the alchemy of his mind, quick to believe, and slow to suspect or distrust, generous and tender to others, in so far as his thought and imagination, which are the weakest things about him, enable him to bridge the spaces that separate man from man, willing to make of life a great thing while he has it, and a little thing when he comes to lose it. These are some of his gifts; and Shakespeare would not have denied the saying of a thinker with whom he has no very strong or natural affinity, that 'the greatest of these is charity'.